MODERN CAMBRIDGE ECONOMICS

ASPECTS OF DEVELOPMENT
AND UNDERDEVELOPMENT

MODERN CAMBRIDGE ECONOMICS

Editors   Phyllis Deane
            Gautam Mathur
            Joan Robinson

Also in the series

Phyllis Deane
The Evolution of Economic Ideas

Michael Ellman
Socialist Planning

ASPECTS OF DEVELOPMENT AND UNDERDEVELOPMENT

Joan Robinson

CAMBRIDGE UNIVERSITY PRESS

CAMBRIDGE
LONDON · NEW YORK · MELBOURNE

Published by the Syndics of the Cambridge University Press
The Pitt Building, Trumpington Street, Cambridge CB2 1RP
Bentley House, 200 Euston Road, London NW1 2DB
32 East 57th Street, New York NY 10022, USA
296 Beaconsfield Parade, Middle Park, Melbourne 3206, Australia

First published 1979

Printed in Great Britain by The Anchor Press Ltd
and bound by Wm Brendon & Son Ltd
both of Tiptree, Essex

Library of Congress Cataloguing in Publication Data
Robinson, Joan, 1903–
Aspects of development and underdevelopment.
(Modern Cambridge economics)
Includes index.
1. Underdeveloped areas. 2. Economic development.
I. Title
HC59.7.R56   330.9′172′4   78–25610
ISBN 0 521 22637 6 hard cover
ISBN 0 521 29589 0 paperback

SERIES PREFACE

The modern Cambridge Economic series, of which this book is one, is designed in the same spirit as and with similar objectives to the series of Cambridge Economic Handbooks launched by Maynard Keynes soon after the First World War. Keynes' series, as he explained in his introduction, was intended 'to convey to the ordinary reader and to the uninitiated student some conception of the general principles of thought which economists now apply to economic problems'. He went on to describe its authors as, generally speaking, 'orthodox members of the Cambridge School of Economics' drawing most of their ideas and prejudices from 'the two economists who have chiefly influenced Cambridge thought for the past fifty years, Dr Marshall and Professor Pigou' and as being 'more anxious to avoid obscure forms of expression than difficult ideas'.

This series of short monographs is also aimed at the intelligent undergraduate and interested general reader, but it differs from Keynes' series in three main ways: first in that it focuses on aspects of economics which have attracted the particular interest of economists in the post Second World War era; second in that its authors, though still sharing a Cambridge tradition of ideas, would regard themselves as deriving their main inspiration from Keynes himself and his immediate successors, rather than from the neoclassical generation of the Cambridge school; and third in that it envisages a wider audience than readers in mature capitalist economies, for it is equally aimed at students in developing countries whose problems and whose interactions with the rest of the world have helped to shape the economic issues which have dominated economic thinking in recent decades.

Finally, it should be said that the editors and authors of this Modern Cambridge Economics series represent a wider spectrum of economic doctrine than the Cambridge School of Economics to which Keynes referred in the 1920s. However, the object of the series is not to propagate particular doctrines. It is to stimulate students to escape from conventional theoretical ruts and to think for themselves on live and controversial issues.

PHYLLIS DEANE
GAUTAM MATHUR
JOAN ROBINSON

CONTENTS

FOREWORD

This small book does not offer a survey of its huge theme. It is intended rather to throw some light upon the question of why a quarter of a century of 'development' has produced results so different from what was proclaimed to be its object. There is a certain complacency in mainstream economic teaching which is misleading even in its homeland and cruelly deceptive when transferred to the Third World. The tone of the argument is pessimistic. This must be a fault on the right side for it will be pleasant to be surprised if things are going to turn out better than now seems likely.

The basic economic theory which seems to me to be useful is a re-interpretation in post-Keynesian terms of the Classical and Marxian theory of accumulation, distribution and trade. To avoid misunderstanding, the appendix to Chapter 2 explains the manner in which I make use of some Marxian concepts.

At a few points, I refer to Chinese experience by way of contrast with that of the rest of the Third World. China is a controversial subject, more than ever in 1978, but I do not think that anyone would deny that the Chinese method of organising a highly labour-intensive agriculture is more successful than any in the so-called free world.

At various stages in preparing this book I have had a great deal of help from the Director and Fellows of the Centre for Development Studies, at Trivandrum, especially Professor K. N. Raj and Professor Gulati; also from Leila Gulati and from the students on whom I tried out my ideas. I also had many useful criticisms and suggestions from Azizur Rahman Khan, especially in connection with trade policy in Pakistan, discussed in Chapter 6, from Keith Griffin and G. B. Ng, and from colleagues in Cambridge, especially Suzy Paine and Mahmoud Abdel Fadil.

JOAN ROBINSON

Cambridge
  December 1978

MISLEADING LIGHTS

The enormous capability, both for production and destruction, of the so-called developed countries in the modern world makes the economic basis of even the richest and most powerful nations in former times appear non-developed by comparison. Except in the 'Western world' (which now includes Japan) in the last two hundred years, the greatest part of all economic activity everywhere was in producing food; the small surplus of output per man year over the needs of subsistence had to be extracted and amassed to provide for urban life, government, warfare and for luxury, of which the greater part was provided by personal services. Industrial capitalism, emerging out of commercial capitalism, proved to be the vehicle for the application of science to technology, which has led, for good or ill, to the unprecedented level of civilian wealth and military force in the Western nations today. The rest of the world (which was largely dominated by European empires before the industrial revolution began) contributed to the growth of capitalism by providing it with sources of supply of a number of animal, mineral and vegetable products, and a labour force to exploit them.

After the first world war, USSR, and after the second, China, seceded from capitalism and began to show that it is not the only economic system which is capable of benefiting from the application of scientific technology to production. The Third World consists of these countries which are attempting to carry out development while remaining within the sphere of the capitalist world market.

History and geography have brought into existence today a great number of independent states of a variety of shapes and sizes which bear no relation to economic potentialities, but the mere fact that they are recognised as states causes them to be regarded by themselves and each other as economic entities. The very concept of political economy grew up in western Europe out of the rivalry of national states and it has been passed over, without question, to the would-be developing states of today, so that the concept of national identity has been built into the ideology of 'development'. A national government is the only authority which can decide upon economic policy and negotiate with other authorities. Many of the newly established states in the Third World won independence through a national struggle against an imperialist administration, which led, not only intellectuals but everyone, to think of themselves in national terms. A large part of the drive behind the movement for economic development is not merely economic, but aims to build up a nation that will be taken seriously in the councils of the world. Statistics are collected and surveys made in the form of comparisons between nations.

There is another class of economic entities besides nations in the contemporary world market, that is, the great transnational corporations. Any one corporation has an annual flow of receipts exceeding the total income of many nations. Each corporation has its base in one of the highly developed countries (most in USA) and expects some protection from its government, but they are not strictly a part of any one national economy. Each draws profits from a variety of operations all over the free-market world and employs a labour force drawn from many countries. Managers and staff owe allegiance to the company that employs them more than to any national authority; their aim is to make profits, nominally for their owners and shareholders, but in reality for the corporation as such, with which their personal fortunes are bound up. There are, no doubt, conflicts and power struggles within corporations, but, in general, their adminstration is far better integrated and their policies much more coherent than those of any nation, which enables them to play an important part in the development and under-development of the Third World.

The Western powers, particularly the United States, exercise a powerful influence over the policies of Third World governments, directly and through international institutions such as the World Bank and the International Monetary Fund which they dominate, as well as through the all-pervasive ramifications of international finance. Along with this goes penetration of their cultural and intellectual life, in particular, the dissemination of a system of economic thought which is orthodox in the West.

Many Western doctrines have been challenged even in their homeland. Our business here is to attempt to examine their validity and the manner in which they have been applied to the problems of the would-be developing world.

Income and welfare

Western teaching pretends to be scientific and objective by detaching the economic aspect of human life from its political and social setting; this distorts the problems that it has to discuss rather than illuminating them.

A leading example of this tendency in the discussion of so-called development is the habit of concentrating upon the concept of Gross National Product, that is a measure of the flow of output, in a particular country, of physical exchangeable goods and services, summed up at market prices, and treating its growth as the object of policy and the criterion of success.

There are many statistical difficulties and philosophical puzzles in the calculation of national income even for a highly organised and highly commercialised Western society; in large sectors of the Third World, the information simply does not exist; tables of comparative GNP have to be filled in with imaginative estimates. The main point, however, is not the difficulty of estimating and comparing national incomes but the very conception itself. What is the meaning of calculating the magnitude of a flow of physical output without regard to its conditions of production or its distribution between the people concerned?

The problem of the distribution of 'national income' and wealth between families that the nation comprises runs deep into the moral confusion at the base of modern Western doctrines. The classical economists took class for granted and treated the needs of subsistence for the 'labouring poor' as part of the cost of production of national wealth; the so-called neoclassical doctrines which came into fashion in the West in the last quarter of the nineteenth century, purported to be more humane and democratic – everyone should count for one. The economists were living, all the same, in a class society in which property dominated over work as a source of consuming power and they were trying to represent its operations in a morally acceptable light. Thus they were caught in a contradiction impossible to resolve.

Alfred Marshall, a great moraliser, observed that a shilling spent by a poor man purchases more *utility* or satisfaction than a shilling spent by a rich man.[1] Yet as the argument goes on, we are imperceptibly led to regard the flow of national income in a private enterprise economy as a flow of utilities, and the flow of utilities as a flow of physical output. This line of escape from the dilemma is commonly followed in discussions of development. The concept of national product as a measure of welfare is an important element in the orthodox economic doctrine which affects the views of Western-style advisers who intend to be helpful to would-be developing countries. For instance, in an influential document, *Guidelines for Project Evaluation*,[2] invest-ment projects are evaluated according to the contribution that each is expected to make to aggregate consumption, and the benefit from consumption is evaluated by 'willingness to pay' that is by the prices at which the incremental flow of output will be sold.

The authors of the document make any number of reservations about the meaning of this measure, and they recognise that 'willingness to pay' must depend mainly on the level of income of the purchaser, but they do not give any other guidance to the advisers who are to help governments judge the merits of possible investment projects. No doubt governments accept this kind of advice readily enough, for they have absorbed the idea that the growth of GNP is the proper object for economic policy, quite irrespective of its content.

The transnational corporations, unlike national authorities, have no need to enter into such metaphysical arguments. They are adept above all in salesmanship. They generate 'willingness to pay' for what they find it convenient to produce and they have no need to be concerned about the meaning of welfare for they

[1] *Principles of Economics,* 8th edition, p. 95.
[2] United Nations Industrial Development Organisation, 1972. It is stated in the Preface that: 'This publication represents the cumulative experience of UNIDO in the methodology and practice of national benefit – cost analysis.

operate on the simple maxim that what is profitable is right.

To evade the dilemma posed by the doctrine that everyone should count for one, it is usual to take refuge in the calculation of averages. Thus GNP *per capita* is treated as the measure of economic success. Nations are arranged in a hierarchy in terms of GNP *per capita*; their wealth and, by implication, the welfare of their inhabitants, is judged in these terms and growth of GNP *per capita* is regarded as the objective of development.

In spite of all the problems involved in aggregating output in terms of market prices, statistical information is certainly valuable (particularly to corporations looking out for profitable fields for investment) but from the point of view of welfare, information about *average* income is meaningless unless we know how consuming power is distributed. A rate of growth of GNP *per capita* of 1 or 2 per cent per annum (which many countries experienced in the first so-called Decade of Development) appears pitiful, but where there has been an increase in inequality and a fall in the proportion of necessaries in the flow of production, 1 or 2 per cent gives a very flattering picture of the actual course of development.

The modernisation of poverty

The contrast between national wealth and human welfare is seen at its most striking in the countries whose export revenues were sharply increased by the rise in the price of oil at the end of 1973.[3] For several of the Arab states, GNP *per capita* suddenly jumped to levels which exceed that of the richest Western states, yet in these countries are found some of the poorest and least 'developed' communities in the world.[4] Oil is a highly exaggerated example of a phenomenon that is general all over the world. In most countries there is a sector linked to world trade and to industry which supports a relatively wealthy urban community; this attracts the destitute from rural life, hoping to find some means to live on the crumbs that fall from the rich man's table.

This is exacerbated by the growth of population. A sharp rise in the rate of growth of numbers has set in in most of the

[3] See below, p. 76.
[4] Cf. Galal Amin, *The Modernisation of Poverty*, E. J. Brill, Leiden, 1974.

countries of the Third World, and, in almost all of them, employment has been growing over the last twenty years less rapidly
than population. Agriculture fails to provide even the barest
livelihood for new generations of would-be cultivators, while the
number of jobs in regular industry and commerce expands slowly.
A flow of dispossessed families has drifted into shanty towns and
slums or on to the streets of cities, living on a physical and social
standard of existence at the limit of human endurance.

The shanty dwellers are sometimes described as living in
'disguised unemployment' but it is better to regard them as self-
employed, with minute quantities of capital, providing communal
and personal services to each other and to their prosperous neighbours, or working in small family businesses or for any amongst
them who have acquired enough finance to employ those more
wretched than themselves.

Economists speculate about this so-called 'informal' employment and debate the question whether it should be included in
the statistics of national income. This is typical of economic
analysis, which concerns itself with physical products, not with
people. Informal business arises from the obstinate desire of
human beings to remain alive. The shanty dwellers, having no
'formal' source of income, make a little money in any way they
can. Where capitalist enterprise does not yet cover the ground,
there are openings for self-employment in providing indispensable
services, without which urban life would be impossible.[5]

Some 'informal' activity may be considered parasitical or even
criminal, but this is not unknown also in 'formal' occupations. It
does not contribute much to physical production, apart from some
scraps of small-scale manufacturers. If GNP is calculated according to the Soviet definition, which includes only physical output,[6]
it would be reasonable to exclude the 'informal' sector but
Western-style GNP includes services, measured at market values.
By this criterion, the income of shanty dwellers measures the
value of the services they perform. (Even beggars provide the
service of allowing their fellow citizens to feel charitable.) Informal earnings have just as good a claim to be included in GNP

---

[5] Cf. *Employment, Incomes and Equality in Kenya,* ILO, p. 5; and
H. Lubell, *Calcutta,* ILO, p. 25.

[6] See below, p. 36.

(if the statistics could be collected) as those of other retailers, or of self-employed members of professions to which entry is limited by the need for certificates of education.

Intense competition in a narrow market keeps the earnings of 'informal' workers low. The fact that they are obliged to provide services at a cheap rate increases the purchasing power of money for their fellow citizens. This leads to a conflict of interest within the formal sphere. Managers of department stores and super-markets object to petty traders who take custom from them while manufacturers find that they provide an outlet for their products at very low profit margins and tap a level of the market that posh and expensive shops cannot reach. This is just as much part of 'national income' as any other element in the market economy.

Spokesmen for the Third World like to deploy comparisons of figures of national income *per capita* in order to demonstrate the difference between rich and poor countries, but there is nowadays great disillusionment with statistical GNP as the objective of development.

Economic growth, where it has occurred, seldom succeeded in making a serious dent in urgent social problems and has too often by-passed the mass of the population in the developing countries. By increasing economic disparities and failing to relieve such problems as unemployment, mal-nutrition, sickness and bad housing, economic growth has served not seldom to aggravate social problems and tensions.[7]

The main requirement now is declared to be 'a frontal attack on mass poverty and unemployment', yet no one seems ready to abandon the misleading economic theories that led to their former illusions.

Population

The 'population explosion' in the present century is generally attributed to medical achievements inhibiting the spread of mass diseases and to a fall in infant mortality due to improved hygiene. An increase in the expectation of life is a clear gain but an increase in the number of bodies in a given territory is by no means an unambiguous benefit. A higher density of settlement (above a threshold, that is soon passed, permitting adequate

[7] UNCTAD IV TD/183, p. 19.

mastery over the environment) means a lower average availability, per family, of natural resources, including cultivatable land, and it becomes progressively more onerous to make good the deficit by investment as density increases. Furthermore, a growth of numbers, starting from any initial level, requires the provision of additional resources which, for a stationary population, could be devoted to improving equipment, education and amenities for those who have been born already.

There is a political, as well as a technical element in the problem. In a society where 'everyone counts for one' the general standard of life would depend upon average wealth, but in a class society (whether feudal or capitalist) a growth of numbers is advantageous to the owners of property. It provides them with more people to exploit, as tenants, servants, slaves or workers, and cuts off the possibility of their escaping into vacant land.

Marx, in his desire to combat the reactionary doctrines of Malthus, did not stress the point that growth of population, under capitalism, is inimical to the interests of the working class, though his own theory clearly indicates that this is the case. When capital accumulation goes on faster than the labour force is growing, the reserve army of the unemployed is absorbed and competition between capitalists for hands causes real wage rates to rise. The consequent reduction in the share of profit in the proceeds of industry slows down accumulation, and when numbers continue to grow, the reserve army is replenished and wages fall again. When the labour force is not growing, accumulation takes the form of technical change which raises output per man employed. Then organised labour can catch a share in the growth of productivity by raising real-wage rates. This, indeed, has happened in the Western economies. The moral seems clear, but some fanatically dogmatic Marxists have joined with the Pope in refusing to admit that the growth of population, in modern conditions, is an impediment to the growth of human welfare. They are siding, against their own convictions, with the nationalistic sentiment which makes each country want to compete with its neighbours in numbers and fill up the space within its boundaries, whatever they may happen to be, and with the Third World capitalists who have no objection to seeing the reserve army of unemployment continuously maintained.

The intellectuals of the Third World, for a long time, tried to avert their eyes from the menace of population growth and they naturally reacted indignantly to the often brutal propaganda emanating from the West on this subject. Nowadays the desirability of reducing birth rates is generally acknowledged in Asia and parts of Latin America (for Africa the problem still lies in the future).

Historically, a fall in infant mortality has been followed by a fall in the birth rate, but historically it has been accompanied by a rise in the general standard of life, some degree of emancipation of women and a spread of education. Changes in law and the invention of gadgets follow rather than cause the desire to limit births.

In modern conditions (not only in the Third World) people living in a disintegrating society have been pushed below the level of calculation and foresight. Amongst those who are keeping their heads above water, there is generally a strong desire to be succeeded by children, particularly sons, to provide security for old age. In most countries in the Third World, infant mortality has fallen enough to generate a population explosion but not yet enough to give assurance to the individual family that they will be able to rear the babies that they have; they want to have many children to be sure of being left with a few. Moreover, in peasant households, children become an economic asset from an early age, being used for minor jobs such as minding cattle and collecting fuel. In this situation, propaganda for family planning is not likely to be very effective. Violent measures, such as were attempted in India in 1976, are likely to be counter-productive. There are some signs, in some regions, that the growth rate has begun to decline, but any growth rate above zero is so much to the bad.

In China a population explosion set in with the restoration of peace and good order after Liberation. There was a thoroughgoing land reform and the beginning of industrialisation; society, within a few years, was organised in such a way that everyone had the opportunity to earn an income and contribute to the national economy; growth of population, therefore, did not generate squalor and misery, but all the same, even today, it is laying a burden on the economy. After some vacillation, the

Chinese authorities embarked on a campaign to get down the birth rate – late marriage and small families – while providing a system of social security and of pensions, which relieves the worst pressure upon families to provide themselves with heirs, and a universal health service. But even if the campaign were completely successful, numbers would still be growing for a long time because of a great bulge in the age composition of the population due to the earlier high birth rate and sharp drop in infant mortality, as well as to a general rise in the length of life. This imposes the need for massive investment in agriculture to increase cultivable land and raise yields so as to provide an increasing flow of agricultural output to keep up with the increase in population.

China has been carrying out a frontal attack on mass poverty and unemployment after dispossessing landlords and nationalising industry. It is not easy to see how the Third World can mount the attack while preserving private property in the means of production and respecting the rules of the free-market economy.

Accumulation

The moralising doctrine which still underlines orthodox Western teaching fails to provide the basis for a theory of economic development because of a confusion in its approach. It identifies the sources of income with 'factors of production'. Each type of income is represented as a 'reward' for the contribution which its recipients make to total output. Thus land rent corresponds to the natural fertility of the soil; wages correspond to the productivity of labour, and interest to the productivity of 'capital'. But does 'capital' mean a supply of productive equipment which assists workers to produce output or does it mean financial property that gives its owner a claim to interest and dividends?

A householder who has inherited wealth or acquired it by saving, or any other means 'moral or immoral, legal or illegal' may be receiving interest on it.[8] Therefore, according to this line of thought, he must be performing a corresponding service. In order to present owning wealth as a productive activity, Marshall described it as 'waiting', that is, postponing expenditure in order

[8] Cf. Marshall, *Principles,* first edition, p. 614.

to enjoy a greater return in the future. The suggestion is that if owners of wealth did not receive interest it would not be worth their while to continue to possess it. Their property would all be consumed at once and then there would be no more capital for industry.

This whole structure of ideas is so unplausible that nowadays it is never set out in plain terms, but the confusion between financial wealth and productive equipment has never been cleared up.

The level of productivity in a national economy does not depend upon the amount of wealth that its citizens have amassed but upon the technology that it has installed, in particular upon the use of energy to supplement human and animal muscle. The highly productive techniques that have been evolved in Western industry require elaborate equipment. This is where 'capital' regarded as stocks of means of production comes into the picture. Obviously, to develop the productivity of an economy requires labour time and other resources to be devoted to increasing the area and fertility of cultivable land, developing sources of energy, improving lines of transport, creating equipment and building up stocks of materials and commodities to permit faster flows of output in the future. In a certain sense, this represents 'national saving' for it requires an excess of production over consumption, but it is the result of economic activity not of owning money. Accumulation requires *finance*. Production takes time but a man must eat every day. Wages have to be paid out in advance, sometimes very long in advance, of returns coming in. The form which accumulation takes depends upon who has control over the finance to carry it out. In the capitalist world, investment and the development of technology (apart from armaments and wars) came about through the pursuit of profit and depended upon the vigour with which competitive accumulation was carried out by private business. In Japan, in one way, and in the Soviet Union in another, a national government took over control of investment and directed it towards overtaking the technical achievements of capitalist industry in order to prevent the nation from being overwhelmed.

In the Third World today, investment is mainly directed by foreign and local profit-seeking enterprises. There have been some attempts at political control over investment 'in the national interest' but the aims of policy have not always been well conceived nor have the measures taken always produced the desired results.

However, national planning is still in fashion among economists and many models are produced showing how growth can be achieved by investment, but this concept of planning is a daydream, for the governments concerned do not in fact have sufficient control over resources to carry plans into effect. As Janos Kornai remarks:

Economy-wide planning models concentrate their attention primarily on 'real' flows such as physical inputs and outputs of the economy, the structure of production, foreign trade, and consumption. The objective of the analysis is to determine numerical, quantitative development targets in these areas. At the same time, these models rarely specify how these goals and targets are to be realised. The models are not particularly instrumental in character. This is one of the most important criticisms made by potential users who feel there is nothing they can do with the results of planning models.[9]

This kind of 'planning' is merely an amusement for theoretical economists. Actual accumulation takes places by organising concrete schemes of investment and providing finance to carry them out.

The planners usually seem to be in a state of confusion through advocating an attempt to imitate the achievements of a planned economy while operating with the theory that accumulation depends upon private saving. In a fully planned economy, the authorities direct resources into production according to the objectives of their policy. The flows of output of consumption goods and services are determined in the plan, while the flow of money income is determined by the level of employment and the pattern of money-wage rates. To balance overall supply and demand there has to be a sufficient excess of money value of goods sold to the public over their money costs (collected in the form of planned profit margins or turnover taxes) to finance the expenses of government, gross investment and free services. (The problem for the planners is to find acceptable types and pro-

---

[9] *Economy Wide Models and Development Planning*, C. R. Blitzer et al. (ed.), p. 24.

portions of output so as to offer to the public a flow of consumption goods that they will want to buy.)

All the same, in an incompletely planned economy, there is a sense in which saving, that is, non-spending of household income, makes an important contribution to growth. More saving by middle class and wealthy households means less expenditure on luxury products, limits the profitability of investment which attracts resources into that sector, and so leaves more available for necessary production. However, the doctrine that unequal distribution of income is helpful to growth because the rich save, is the reverse of the truth for there would be less unnecessary expenditure if they were less rich. By the same token, simple habits of life and the absence of 'conspicuous consumption' are propitious to accumulation. This is not likely to be achieved by first allowing a wealthy class to grow and then appealing to them to save.

Market prices

The most extravagant claim of Western orthodoxy is that the free play of the forces of supply and demand, in competitive conditions, tends to establish an equilibrium pattern of prices for commodities. Here the argument is so excessively abstract as to have no application to any real system of production and exchange. The economy is conceived to consist of an undifferentiated set of individuals each with an 'endowment' of some form of productive capacity and with particular 'tastes' for consumption. Given technical conditions, a position of equilibrium can be described in which the pattern of prices and outputs is such that all markets are cleared and a position established in which no individual could gain an advantage from changing either his offers of production or his outlay for consumption.[10] However, the process by which such a position could be reached has never been satisfactorily described. In recent times, there has been a proliferation of neo-neoclassical models elaborated in mathematical terms but these also are built upon the shaky foundations of timeless equilibrium.

To discuss the formation of the prices of commodities in reality,

[10] For an explanation of the meaning of this theory and of why it is useless, see Janos Kornai, *Anti-equilibrium,* North-Holland, 1971.

it is necessary to distinguish between various ways of organising sales. For manufactured goods it is common practice for the producer to set a price which is calculated to cover costs, with a margin of net profit, on some standard rate of output and to sell from week to week what the market will take at that price. When more than the standard output is being sold, he is making greater than expected profits. In this type of market, prices are found to be sensitive to costs (money-wage rates and purchases of materials) but not to vary much with the level of demand. Production and sales are continuous; there is never a moment when 'the market is cleared'.

Primary products, including the staple agricultural crops, are mainly handled by merchants, who buy to sell again. For seasonal agricultural crops there are regular, foreseeable price movements over the year. The peasant must sell as soon as he can. Merchants buy up the crop at harvest time at the lowest price and sell out stocks as the price rises over the year. A rich farmer can hold stocks and enjoy this profit for himself. There are also erratic changes. A shortfall of supply will reduce stocks and causes prices to be raised; unexpectedly slack demand may bring them down. A high price for a particular crop in one season may lead to an increase in output which overshoots and causes the price to crash next year. Certainly, these prices are under the influence of supply and demand, but there is no mechanism to bring the market into equilibrium.

Internal terms of trade

The most important aspect of the pattern of prices is the terms of trade which it establishes between industry and agriculture. Here the economist's vision of the processes of exchange, in competitive conditions, as a scene of harmony and self-regulating stability is highly misleading, for there is an inescapable conflict of interest between the members of the two sectors of an economy. A rise in the relative price of agricultural produce favours the rural population as a whole at the expense of the city. But there are also conflicts within each sector; agricultural workers whose wages are fixed in terms of money suffer from a rise in the price of grain which benefits their employers.

Moreover, the economist's theory does not explain what an equilibrium pattern of relative prices would be. (It could apply only to a world without change – an ideal stationary state – where conditions have always remained the same and are expected to continue to remain the same in the future.) In the conditions of a free market, the terms of trade are constantly changing. The supply of agricultural products is generally *inelastic* in the sense that a rise in prices cannot call forth, before a year has passed, a commensurate increase in sales. At the same time, demand is inelastic, in the sense that a rise in prices of foodstuffs does not cause purchases to be reduced proportionately. An increase in industrial employment, which raises demand in the cities, is liable to bring about a sharp rise in the price of foodstuffs. On the other tack, a good crop, when demand is constant, actually reduces the purchasing power of rural income. (This is the case of the farmer who hanged himself in the expectation of plenty.)

In fact, the internal terms of trade are too important to be left to the free play of market forces and everywhere they are manipulated politically. In the successful capitalist countries, support prices are used to give agriculture a fair share in the national income. The burden is thrown upon industry; employers and employed are left to fight out how it is to be distributed between real-wage rates and profits. In the Third World, where industrialisation is taking place in a mainly agricultural setting, prices are manipulated politically. Often the landed interest is favoured by high procurement prices for the main crops, while some attempt is made to soften the blow to the urban workers by subsidising sales of foodstuffs.

The conflict of interest between town and country exists equally in a planned economy, but there prices are more or less successfully controlled, and the terms of trade are not allowed to be influenced by the vagaries of the market.[11] In the Soviet style model, as the industrial labour force grows, the necessary transfer from agriculture is assisted, up to a certain point, by a movement in terms of trade favourable to industry, so that a larger amount of grain is exchanged against the product of a smaller amount of industrial labour, but when the movement is pushed too far it

[11] Cf. M. Abdel–Fadil, *La Planification des Prix — Economic Socialist* (Paris : Presses Universitaires de France, 1975), Ch. VI.

defeats itself, for however agriculture may be organised, it is not easy to get the cultivator to exchange his crops for money when there is nothing for him to spend money on. The Chinese policy has been to raise agricultural prices gradually while reducing the prices of manufactures as productivity increases, thus continuously improving the terms of trade for agriculture.

International terms of trade

The so-called theory of international trade is even less useful for analysing relative prices than the theory of equilibrium in a competitive market.[12] Following the narrow groove of the traditional argument against protection, the theory is usually confined to a case in which the trading countries potentially or actually produce the same commodities. This cannot be applied to exchanges of primary products with manufactures. The resources of what is now the Third World were developed by the imperialist countries precisely because they were not available at home. Most of the Third World countries have to rely for export earnings on one or a few particular primary commodities. Here, once more, the free play of market forces, far from tending to equilibrium, produces continuous short-term instability as well as unpredictable changes in the terms of trade from time to time. Since the main purchasers of many primary products are in the Western industrialised countries, the division of interest between buyers and sellers is seen as running along national boundaries.

Spokesmen for the Third World have developed the theory of unequal exchange.[13] As accumulation and technical change go on in industry in modern conditions, the workers in the capitalist countries are in a strong enough bargaining position to secure a share for themselves. As the value of output per head rises, money-wage rates rise at least proportionately, so that prices do not fall. In primary production, an increase in productivity leads to a fall in selling prices, in competitive conditions, unless there has been a proportionate increase in demand. Thus, even when the terms of trade reckoned in commodities are fairly constant, it is easy

[12] Cf. below, p. 103.
[13] Cf. Arghiri Emmanuel, *Unequal Exchange,* New Left Books, London, 1972.

to show that the terms of trade reckoned in labour time exhibit a strong and continuous movement against the primary producers. This argument challenges the complacency of those economists who imply that the free play of the market can be relied upon to distribute the benefits of trade between the participants in some sense 'efficiently' so that it is beneficial to all, but there is nothing either in orthodox or in Marxian economics to explain what an efficient pattern of prices would be.

According to the thesis of unequal exchange, not only the capitalists but also the workers in the industrial countries are taking an unfair advantage of trade with the Third World. Western trade-union leaders resent this suggestion. Their members do not compare their earnings with those of miserable workers and peasants abroad but with the profits in the industry where they are employed. They regard it as right and proper to fight to keep their share in proceeds from falling, and they are very reluctant to admit that, through the terms of trade, their gains are partly at the expense of low incomes elsewhere.

Here again, thinking in terms of *national* income confuses the issue. For instance, the drastic change in terms of trade brought about by OPEC caused a sharp rise of GNP for its members (while it was a blow to those countries in the Third World that do not have oil of their own) but it appears that not much of the benefit has yet accrued to the peasants and workers in the nations concerned.[14] It seems that, not only in the West, the calculation of GNP *per capita* is a smoke screen to keep the problems of distribution out of view.

[14] See Galal Amin, op. cit.

2

SURPLUS AND ACCUMULATION

The moralising neoclassical doctrines came into fashion after Marx had developed from the theories of classical economists, particularly Ricardo, an interpretation of capitalism as a system of exploitation. The neoclassicals attempted to oppose to this a theory of 'factors of production' each receiving its just reward, but, as we have seen, they did not succeed in making this convincing. It is better to abandon that line of thought and return to the classics to see how their conceptions can be adapted to deal with our contemporary problems.

Rent as surplus

In the eighteenth century in France, the doctrines of the Physiocrats laid the foundation of economic theory by presenting the flow of production and consumption of material goods as a self-reproducing system yielding a surplus over necessary costs. (The Mercantilist school which preceded them, concentrating upon overseas trade, had many sharp insights but no comprehensive frame of ideas in which to embody them.)

The Physiocrats accepted as normal a class structure dominated by a land-owning aristocracy but by concentrating upon the conditions favourable to production they prepared the way for the doctrines of liberal capitalism which succeeded the French Revolution. They treated agricultural rent as the *net product* of an economy as a whole and regarded it as measuring the productivity of land. The cultivators owned a certain stock of working capital, sufficient to provide seed and other inputs and the annual consumption of their families. This stock was continuously reconstituted out of the year's production as it was used up. The surplus yielded by the land was the excess of output over its cost of production, including the consumption of the cultivators as part of costs. The products of artisans – handicraftsmen – were sold at prices which, reckoned in terms of agricultural products, just covered their costs and yielded no surplus. The excess of each harvest over the necessary level of consumption of the cultivators for the following year was handed over to the landlords as rent. This they disposed of in purchases from artisans, payments for domestic and professional services and in supporting the civil and military apparatus of the state. By this means, the surplus product of agriculture was put at the disposal of the rest of the economy.

In the system of the Physiocrats, the problem of marketing output is left to solve itself. Rent is paid in kind. The consumption of each peasant family is mainly from its own produce, though they may make some swaps amongst themselves or with artisans. It is tacitly assumed that the value of sales by artisans to peasants and landlords is just sufficient to permit them to maintain the same customary standard of life as the peasants.

Historically it is true that the supplies required for urban civilisation and military power have been taken, without return, from the product of cultivation, in the form of land rent or tribute to the state. This mechanism is still at work in a large part of the Third World. But it is not true that the generation of surplus is a purely technical relationship; there is no hard and fast division between the product of the soil and the product of work applied to it. What can be extracted as surplus depends upon the structure of society, legal rights of property and the power of the state to enforce them.

The upper limit to the flow of produce that can be extracted depends upon the flow of net output and upon the consumption of the cultivators who produce it, and both these quantities vary widely according to circumstances. Output depends upon natural conditions and the technique of production while consumption depends upon social relations. There is no definite minimum below which the cultivators' consumption cannot fall. Demographic relationships are a major influence on distribution. As numbers seeking employment grow, the bargaining power of landowners is enhanced. Rents rise and the share of produce going to the cultivator is squeezed. Many tenants are unable to support their families out of their share in one harvest and borrow in order to live until the next. Then the burden of usury is added to rent and squeezes their consumption still further. The interest paid to moneylenders is subtracted from the income of the cultivator, not added to the flow of production. So long as this use of funds yields a substantial return there is no motive to risk them in productive investment.

Surplus as profit

In the Physiocrats' model there is no capital and no distinction between wages and profits. Cultivators and artisans each manage their own work according to traditional methods and are responsible for maintaining the stocks of equipment and other inputs that their various operations require. Adam Smith, later in the eighteenth century, after capitalist industry had begun to spread in England, carried the argument into a new sphere. He took it for granted that workers were employed for wages and that their masters organised business. This enlarged the concept of surplus to include commerce and manufactures. He conceived the contribution of industry to surplus product to correspond to the net profit accruing to employers. This depends, first, upon output per man employed and, second, upon the relation of the selling price of the product to the money wage per man.

Adam Smith was well aware of the political element in the determination of surplus. He regarded land rent as an exaction corresponding to no service to society and he remarked that employers were constantly conspiring together to raise prices and keep down wages, while workers were forbidden by law to combine for their own defence. At the same time, the extraction of profit permitted the employment of workers in large units which brought about economies through division of labour and so contributed to an ever-growing flow of surplus product. Thus his attitude was ambivalent. On the one side, he maintained that all wealth is produced by work; the landlord and the capitalist muscle in and take part of the product for themselves. On the other side, it is the capitalists' search for profits that causes labour to be organised in such a way as to provide the increase of national wealth.

The neoclassics claim Adam Smith as their patron because he

was an advocate of laisser faire. He believed in freeing the ener-
gies of self-interested action from limitations and restrictions by
the state but he was not concerned with equilibrium; the famous
invisible hand[1] is not directing the allocation of scarce means
between alternative uses, but guiding investment into the most
advantageous channels and so promoting the growth of means
to employ more labour and create more wealth.

In general, demand was expected to grow in step with output,
but for any particular commodity there might be a temporary
deficiency or excess which would be cured by a fall or rise in its
relative price.

Adam Smith drew a distinction between productive and
unproductive labour. He was not concerned with problems of
measurement but with the process of generation of surplus. The
labour of a worker in a factory produces goods that sell for more
than his wage and so contributes to his master's profit, whereas
the labour of a personal servant is paid for out of profits rather
than enhancing them.

In modern conditions, when so many kinds of services have
been commercialised, the distinction is not always easy to draw.
For instance, Adam Smith regarded the work of buffoons and
opera singers as unproductive but nowadays the entertainments
industry is certainly a source of profit.

However, we may follow Adam Smith in regarding administration and defence as unproductive :

The sovereign for example, with all the officers both of justice and war who
serve under him, the whole army and navy, are unproductive labourers.
They are the servants of the public, and are maintained by a part of the
annual produce of the industry of other people.[2]

However honourable, useful or necessary these services may be,
they are consuming the surplus, like private luxury, and reducing
the potential growth of wealth.

Rent and profits

Ricardo treated surplus as consisting of two separate parts,
rent and profits. He regarded landed property as an incubus
upon society because rent was consumed in luxury. The function

---

[1] *Wealth of Nations*, Book IV, Chapter II.
[2] *Wealth of Nations*, Book II, Chapter III.

of profits was to be saved and invested in increasing employment and production. As employment expands, in a given territory, the areas of land taken into cultivation are successively less fertile or less convenient to work, so that average output per man employed grows less. Competition for the better land drives up rents; the necessary wage per man-year is taken as given and cannot be reduced. Thus profits are squeezed as output expands.

Ricardo's analysis of rent gave rise to the concept of the marginal productivity of labour. At any stage in the process of expansion there is some land, at the margin of cultivation, which is yielding the lowest output per man; so long as there is still vacant land of no worse quality, rent cannot be charged for the marginal land. In principle, the level of rents of better lands has been pushed to the point where it is a matter of indifference to the farmer whether he employs an addition to his labour force by taking in no-rent land or by increasing the intensity of cultivation on better land, for which he is paying rent consonant with its quality. Thus internal and external margins of productivity are equalised. At any given ratio of labour to land, there is a particular marginal productivity of labour, being the difference between the total output due to n man-years of work deployed over the given territory minus the output of $n-1$ man-years. It is to be observed that this marginal productivity is nothing to do with the determination of the wage rate; it is the essence of Ricardo's system that the wage in terms of product is given independently of the amount of employment or the average product per man.

On the same basis, Ricardo found out a theory of the determination of the rate of profit on investment; this was lost to view, overlaid by the neoclassical concept of the productivity of capital, until it was disinterred and brought to light by Piero Sraffa.[3]

The stock which the capitalist farmer requires to employ workers on the land, neglecting equipment such as ploughs and inputs such as fertilisers, Ricardo treated as essentially consisting of corn – the standard type of grain whatever it may be – retained from the last harvest to provide seed and pay out as wages week

---

[3] 'Introduction' to the *Principles of Political Economy and Taxation. Works and Correspondence of David Ricardo, Vol.* 1 Cambridge University Press, 1952.

by week over the coming year. The fund of wages required per man employed is then a function of the wage in terms of corn and the turnover period, which is given by nature – a year from harvest to harvest. The output of a man-year of work on marginal land is a quantity of corn. (This is equal to the gross product minus rent on all other land.) From output, subtract the year's wage bill and seed required to employ a man next year. What remains is the surplus or net output. This constitutes the farmer's profit. The rate of profit on capital is then the ratio of the surplus, as a flow of corn being produced, to the self-replacing stock of corn invested in production.

When competition among capitalists has established a more or less uniform rate of profit throughout industry, prices are such that each employer is paying a wage in terms of his own product that has the same purchasing power over the corn that his workers consume. Thus the level of the rate of profit in industry is determined by the conditions of production in agriculture.

Obviously this analysis is extremely simplified and stylised. Both means of production and real wages contain a variety of ingredients besides corn. All the same, it illustrates an important principle. The rate of profit that can be realised in the production of wage goods sets the standard for all the rest and this rate of profit is determined by the technical conditions of production and the share of wages in net output.

This is the basis of the alternative theory of distribution which challenges the neoclassical concept of the 'marginal productivity of capital'.

Ricardo himself got lost in what is nowadays called the problem of aggregation. He recognised that wage goods are not really just a quantity of corn and that the stock of inputs necessary to provide employment is not just a wage fund. It was no good operating in terms of money prices, for prices are obviously not independent of the level of the rate of profit. Till his dying day, he was searching for an invariable measure of value, like a measure of length or weight,[4] which would enable him to express output, wages, capital and profits as quantities in terms of a precise unit, so that the relations between them could be expressed as simply as though they were all quantities of corn.

[4] *Absolute Value and Exchangeable Value. Works,* Vol. IV.

B

Ricardo was the first consciously to confront the problem of overall effective demand that is, of a sufficient flow of expenditure to purchase all that is produced for sale. In his argument with Malthus,[5] he denied that it is a problem. He assumed that landlords spend rents and workers spend wages currently as they are received. Capitalists may spend a small part of their receipts for their families' consumption; all the rest is continuously reinvested in their businesses; thus net investment automatically absorbs net saving and there can be no problem of a deficiency of demand for output until the rate of profit has fallen, because of the rising share of rent, to such a low level that it does not cover the trouble and risk of further investment.

Marxian value

Marx incorporated Ricardo's economic analysis in his treatment of the historical and political evolution of society. Capitalism is a particular economic system that grew out of feudalism. It will develop through the interplay of the contradictions in its own internal structure, which in due course will destroy it and bring a new society to birth.

The clash of interests, which Ricardo saw between industrial capitalists and landlords, had been largely resolved in favour of industry by Marx's time. His central theme was the far more persistent and deep-seated conflict between the interests of the owners of property in the means of production and of the dispossessed workers who have no way to live except by taking service with them.

Marx's description of the evolution of capitalism is complex, rich and detailed, illustrated by much factual evidence, mainly from English sources, but there is a simplified model at the core of the argument. Industrial production is going on in a two-class society, composed of workers and capitalists. The ouput of commodities, that is goods produced for sale, is measured by their *value*, the labour time directly and indirectly required to produce them. For Marx, the concept of *value* was a profound philosophical insight into the nature of capitalism and it carries a heavy weight of ideological implications. At the same time, in

[5] *Works,* Volumes II and VII.

the model, measuring output in terms of his conception of *value* provides a solution for the aggregation problem, though difficulties remain about the *value* generated by skilled and professional work compared to that of the ordinary standard labour which provides the basic unit.

The 'labour theory of value' does not mean that a man can produce anything with his bare hands. Marx insisted upon the necessity for a pre-existing stock of means of production on which the worker operates. In the formula for the flow of *value* created per annum, $c + v + s$, c represents the labour time embodied in the stocks of materials which are used up in production over a year and the wear and tear of equipment. This is added to the value produced during the year, $v + s$, which is measured by the sum of man hours of labour annually performed, divided between the part, v, the *value* of the wages paid to workers and the surplus, s, which accrues to capitalists. This formulation makes it possible to concentrate on Marx's main preoccupation – s/v – the rate of exploitation or the ratio of surplus to wages.

When capitalists first begin to compete with the products of self-employed artisans, they have to offer real wages which provide more or less the existing standard of life. The labour *value* of these wage goods is the *value of labour power*. By collecting workers in factories and subjecting them to discipline, employers oblige them to work longer and harder than the self-employed would have been willing to do for the same earnings. By cutting the wage of the breadwinner, women and children are driven to work. Thus more *surplus value* is squeezed out per unit of wages. The spread of capitalism deprives more and more families of their own means of production so that workers, in Marx's sarcastic phrase, become 'free labour'. When the peasant and artisan economy has been destroyed the whole labour force is fairly caught. Then the level of real wages can be depressed by raising prices or cutting money-wage rates and the share of *surplus value* in net output raised all the more. The forces of law and order back up employers by penalising leaders who attempt to protest, inhibiting labour organisations and preventing strikes.

As industrialisation progresses, output per man is raised and it becomes possible to concede higher real wages without reducing profits. Spokesmen for the workers, backed up by general humanitarian sentiment, begin to demand legal protection. (In England, the first victory was a limitation on hours of work for women.[6]) Enlightened employers begin to realise that by degrading the labour force they are sawing off the bough that they are sitting on. They break ranks with their class-fellows and support reforms. In the end, trade unions become a recognised element in the institutional apparatus of capitalism.

The formal model, with a clear-cut distinction between gross and net output and a single overall rate of exploitation, is too simple to display all the variety of the Marxian interpretation of the history of industrial capitalism in the West; the scene in the Third World today is still more varied, but the model provides a framework which can be adapted to the analysis of problems of would-be developing countries.*

There modern industry is being, so to say, imported ready-made rather than evolved from within. The process of undercutting and ruining artisans and small businesses is still going on but the main source of the growth of a proletariat divorced from means of production has been due to demography (which Marx neglected) more than to the take-over of agriculture by capitalism, though that is also playing a part in the process.

The small portion of the potential labour force taken into employment in Western-style industry is in a privileged position in relation to the mass of destitution around it. The corporations generally find it convenient to offer wages somewhat above the local average level of incomes. This permits them to recruit the most able and docile workers and cements their loyalty. These workers, however, are not allowed to make demands for themselves. It is noticeable that the most rapid growth of industry in the Third World takes place under highly repressive regimes (though there are also repressive regimes without much growth of industry).

---

* Some controversial points in Marxian analysis are discussed in the appendix below.

[6] See *Capital,* Volume I, Chapter 10.

Accumulation

Marx's treatment of capitalism as a system of exploitation was offensive to the neoclassicals but at the same time he showed that exploitation is the great engine for accumulation and what is nowadays called economic growth.

The capitalists extract *surplus value*, not to enjoy luxury, but to accumulate the means of increasing employment so as to extract more surplus. This theme runs through the whole argument. It is formally set out in the 'schema of expanded reproduction' in Volume II of *Capital*.

Still in the simple two-class model, industry is divided into three departments, characterised by the type of commodities produced, or rather the uses to which they are to be put. Department I produces means of production, that is, *investment goods*. These are acquired by the active capitalists, or entrepreneurs. Department II produces necessaries for consumption, *wage goods*, which go to the workers, and III, *luxuries*, which are consumed by rentiers. Rentier income is derived from profits or dividends, interest on former loans, rents and the allowances that capitalists make for their own household expenditure. The two categories of consumption goods are distinguished not so much by their physical nature as by who buys them. Thus we may treat anything sold to rentiers as a luxury, though there may be some items in common in their pattern of consumption and that of workers.

Instead of outputs being measured in terms of *value*, they may be treated in terms of flows of money incomes and expenditure, taking as the unit of account, say, the monthly wage of an ordinary labourer. (This is a departure from Marx's terminology but, in this context, it does not affect the analysis.)

Since means of production are owned by capitalists, we divide the flow of expenditure into gross profits (corresponding to $c + s$) and wages (corresponding to v). Part of gross profits are expended on the output of department I, to replace and increase the stocks of means of production used in all three departments, and part is expended on the output of department III, luxury consumption. The output of department II is absorbed by the wage bill of all three departments.

When agriculture has been fully drawn into capitalism, it can be treated on the same basis as the rest of the economy. A large part of the expenditure of industrial wages and some part of the expenditure on raw materials can then be regarded as generating profits in agriculture, part of which is absorbed by the rent payable on land. The agricultural surplus in turn is expended upon the products of departments I and III of industry. However, in the existing mixture of capitalist and pre-capitalist conditions in many Third World countries, the problems of extracting a surplus from agriculture are too complicated and too various to be fitted into this simple schematism. We leave them to be discussed in the next chapter.

Here, there is no point in separating services from physical output. It is simpler to regard services as performed along with other work in the departments to which they belong. Thus, shop assistants contribute to department II, while butlers and opera singers contribute to department III. But it is important to distinguish productive from unproductive labour in Adam Smith's sense. The unproductive sector, administration and the armed forces, draws upon all three departments: on department I for armaments and government buildings, on department II for supplies for the troops (who, in the Third World, are usually maintained at a better standard of life than the general run of workers and peasants) and on department III for supplies to the upper ranks of military and civil services. When all these expenses are deducted from the flow of national income, what remains of the surplus, net profits and rent, is divided between expenditure on investment and luxury consumption.

An increase in employment at the pre-existing technological level requires a proportionate increase in the stock of means of production, both to increase capacity for producing wage goods and to provide more equipment to operate.

Two very important considerations, relevant to Third World conditions, are brought out by this argument. First, that investment in capacity to produce wage goods is a necessary condition for growth; second that the funds for investment consist of profits *minus* luxury consumption; for a given share of profits in proceeds, the greater the expenditure on luxuries the slower the rate of growth of the stock of means of production as a whole, and the larger the proportion that will be deflected into providing for the growth of luxury output.

Effective demand

In a one-technique economy, the potential amount of employment depends upon the total stock in existence of means of production and the overall physical capital to labour ratio, but the realisation of the potential amount of employment depends upon the state of effective demand. The amount of output that businesses find it profitable to produce is the amount that they expect to sell for a flow of receipts that exceeds its cost by a sufficient margin.

To see the problem in its simplest form, consider the industrial sector of an economy in isolation, abstracting from the agricultural sector, from government and external trade, and, at the first step, from expenditure on luxury goods (department III). Then the problem is reduced to the question : how is it possible for the capitalists (taken as a whole) to make a profit by selling wage goods to workers whose wages they are paying themselves? The answer is that wages are being paid not only for producing a flow of wage goods but also to workers engaged in investment in replacing and expanding the stock of means of production. The expenditure of these wages provides the excess of the receipts from sales of wage goods over their own wage bill. Part of this excess covers the cost of replacing and expanding means of production (including stock for department II when employment is increasing) which adds to their wealth and to their productive capacity. This is the essential mechanism of exploitation or the extraction of a surplus from the employment of labour.

Expenditure by rentiers leads to employment in department III; its wage bill is an element in profit on the sale of wage goods and the excess of the expenditure over the cost of production is profit in the luxury department. Thus the flow of profits per annum being received by capitalists as a whole is equal to capitalists' annual expenditure on investment and consumption. In terms of *value*, surplus is equal to labour time employed in departments I and III, less the *value* of means of production used up in all three departments; in terms of money income, gross profits are equal to the whole flow of expenditure minus the wage bill. The value of net investment carried out over any period is the excess of income over consumption, that is, the saving made over the period.

An individual capitalist, of course, cannot get profits for himself by his own expenditure. The profits of each depend on the expenditure of all. The amount of investment that an individual capitalist *wants* to undertake, in any period of time, depends on the prospects of profits, as he sees them, from expanding his business and upon the 'animal spirits', or 'greed for *surplus value*' that drives him to go out for them. The amount that he *can* undertake depends upon the finance that he commands, either from the profits of his existing business or from borrowing. A scheme of investment cannot be financed out of the profits that it will yield in the future; it requires to be financed in advance. The availability of finance has an important influence on the rate of accumulation, but the provision of finance is not sufficient by itself to guarantee that investment will be carried out.

An excess of total income over expenditure on consumption, similar to that generated by investment, may be due to an excess of government outlay over receipts (a budget deficit) or to a net excess of receipts from exports over payments for imports (a favourable balance of trade). In the first case, the savings corresponds to an addition to the national debt and, in the second, to a net acquisition of foreign assets including exchange reserves.

Keynes' theory of employment was concerned with a fully developed capitalist economy and the model set out in the *General Theory* was primarily designed to discuss the causes of the rise and fall of employment and the level of utilisation of productive capacity already in existence. This is a different question from the growth of industrial employment in the Third World, but that question also involves the Keynesian principle of effective demand, or in Marxian language, the process of the *realisation of surplus value*. A flow of output cannot be sold at prices in excess of its cost of production, so as to yield profits, unless there is a flow of income to be spent on it in excess of that derived from its own costs.

When all investment is carried out by profit-seeking business (including investment in housing), the budget is balanced and so is the balance of trade, then, if capitalists live up to the imperative 'Accumulate! Accumulate! That is Moses and prophets', there is no problem of effective demand (though there may be any amount of non-employment – the reserve army of labour). All gross profits are continually being invested and all income being expended as it is received. There can be no problem of deficient demand, for firms re-invest their profits simply because they have received them, there is no distribution of profits to rentiers, and there is no difficulty about finance, because there is no outside borrowing; each firm carries out investment with its own profits.

As total income increases, there has to be an increase in the stock of money in circulation but this comes about automatically as firms borrow from banks to finance the excess of next week's outlay over the last week's receipts.

In reality, the growth of income falters when firms reduce investment, waiting to see whether it is going to be worth while. Then profits fall below their former level and a slump sets in. This is the most important reason for a decline in effective demand, but there are two subsidiary reasons, arising from the fact that not all profits are invested – part are paid out to rentiers – and not all investment is financed out of a firm's own profits – part is covered by borrowing. Rentiers may reduce expenditure below what the firms expected it to be in an attempt to add to their savings and so cause a decline in the markets for consumption goods, or they may be reluctant to lend to firms (by buying their securities) so that it becomes difficult to finance an excess of investment over retained profits.

A vulgarised version of Keynes' theory, at one time prevalent in the West, is that governments can always make up for a deficiency of demand by spending money, in excess of revenue, on something or other, that is, by running a budget deficit. (In the Western economies, this doctrine was unfortunate as it helped to encourage deficit expenditure on armaments.)

If the government of a would-be developing country which has picked up this theory tries to promote investment just by spending money, it is liable to run into three sets of difficulties. There is little idle capacity in the investment-good industries (department 1) waiting to be used. Schemes have to be started from scratch and they will take a long time to bear fruit. Meanwhile labour is being employed, wages are being paid and food is being bought. When there are no stocks to make supply elastic, there is a rise in the price of food-stuffs that may set off a continuing inflation. Meanwhile profits are being generated, directly and indirectly, by the government outlay. A part comes back in an increased yield of taxes and the rest accrues as savings in the private sector of the economy. These are partly used to finance investment outside the government schemes and partly for buying jewels or to purchase land or foreign assets, rather than for taking up the bonds which the government issues to cover its deficit, so that it becomes progressively harder for the government to borrow the funds that it needs to maintain its expenditure.

Rentier consumption

According to orthodox economic theory, accumulation is due to saving and it is necessary to society to have a wealthy class because only the rich save. Saving may add to the wealth of an individual family but a nation can add to its productive capacity only by investment. The rich are those who maintain a high level of consumption and so eat into the surplus available for investment.

There was already a small wealthy class in every 'underdeveloped' country before 'development' began to be talked about, living from land rent, the profits of trade and the beginnings of industry. They spent their incomes partly upon indigenous luxuries (it is said that in India in the old days, rent in Rajasthan supported elephants and in Bengal, poets), partly on domestic service, and partly on imported Western-style goods.

Over the last twenty years, national incomes in the Third World have been growing and have been, to some extent, supplemented by grants and loans; inequality in the distribution of income between families has generally been increasing so that the flow of purchasing power accruing to wealthy households has been considerably swollen. Consequently the flow of expenditure on Western-style luxuries has increased markedly. Meanwhile there has been a great development of new types of consumption goods in the West – in particular, motor cars and electric gadgets for domestic use. In the West, the growth of real-wage rates and

employment opportunities in industry made house servants too
expensive for all but the super-rich; this created a market for
appliances such as washing machines, refrigerators and air-
conditioners, at first supplied to the middle classes and later
becoming available also to workers' households. In the Third
World, servants are still employed at low wages, while the higher
incomes are spent upon gadgets as well.

Ricardo, looking at an early stage of industrial capitalism,
regarded it as natural that rent should be consumed in luxury
by the landlords maintaining a feudal style of life in their great
houses, while it was natural for capitalists to be frugal. Marx also
believed that the aim of capitalists making profits was to invest
them in order to make more profits, not to spend them on consumption. Keynes described the growth of the European economy
before 1914 as based on 'a double bluff or deception' :

On the one hand the labouring classes accepted from ignorance or power-
lessness, or were compelled, persuaded, or cajoled by custom, convention,
authority, and the well-established order of Society into accepting a situation in which they could call their own very little of the cake, that they and
Nature and the capitalists were cooperating to produce. And on the other
hand the capitalist classes were allowed to call the best part of the cake theirs
and were theoretically free to consume it, on the tacit underlying condition
that they consumed very little of it in practice. The duty of 'saving' became
nine-tenths of virtue and the growth of the cake the object of true religion.[7]

In the Third World, capitalists have been cutting the cake before
the process of accumulation has got fairly under way.

It might be said that, where there is general lack of employment, it is better to work for rentiers than not to work at all.
But, when additions to rentier consumption turn from employing
more servants to buying manufactured goods, they provide less
employment and they absorb other resources as well.

The chief effect of this type of expenditure is to attract investment into increasing productive capacity for the least necessary
kind of production. When income is unequally distributed and
the higher incomes are largely spent on luxury goods, profits are
easier and quicker to make in the markets fed by rentier consumption than in supplying wage goods or in building up the
capacity of basic industry to produce means of production.
Moreover, a large part of the investment that caters for the

[7] *Economic Consequences of the Peace,* 1919, p. 16.

consumption of the rich is not really adding to productive capacity at all; it is merely taking over the market for pre-capitalist handicraft production or from small-scale family businesses, so reducing employment and increasing the inequality of income which keeps its own market expanding.

It is a very remarkable fact that there is no discussion at all in orthodox economics of what form of investment is desirable from the point of view of society. The usual doctrine is that the free play of market forces allocates given resources between alternative uses, but investment is creating resources additional to those already in existence. On what principle are they to be allocated? Keynes was interested in investment mainly as a means of keeping up effective demand and did not much care about its content. In the absence of any analysis of this question, economists generally seem to support the capitalists' principle that what is profitable is right. The application of this principle in the Third World leads to a large part of whatever surplus is available being devoted to the kind of production least propitious to all-round economic progress. Those who benefit from this kind of consumption, and from the profits to be made out of it, have the most political power (along with landlords and capitalist farmers) and they are not likely to be keen on supporting a different type of development.

Conventional measures of GNP *per capita* are used to divide the world into rich and poor countries without paying any attention to the division between rich and poor people within each. In fact, the highest level of luxurious living is often found in the poorest countries and, with it, the greatest concentration of power in the hands of a few.

Appendix

Value and prices. Reckoning in terms of *value* and the rate of exploitation means reckoning with the share of profit in the net proceeds of industry. When competitive accumulation brings about a more or less uniform rate of profit on capital, then the relative prices of commodities (as Ricardo saw) will be proportional to their *values* only if investment per man employed (the capital to labour ratio) is the same in all lines of production.

Marx made heavy weather of working out the 'prices of production' which yield a uniform rate of profit throughout industry. The so-called transformation of *values* into prices has given rise to a great deal of confusing controversy, but it is merely a mathematical puzzle. As Sraffa has shown,[8] the technical conditions of production and the share of wages in net output determine both the rate of profit, giving a set of normal prices for particular outputs, and the corresponding set of *values* – the labour time directly and indirectly required to produce a unit of the respective commodities. Prices are not exactly proportional to *values* but they are systematically related to them according to the level of the rate of profit.

In reality, of course, the rate of profit is never exactly uniform; indeed since, in modern industry, techniques of production and the composition of output are constantly changing, physical inputs used up are generally replaced with something different so that it is impossible to make an exact distinction between gross and net output. It is true that gross profit margins (the ratios of prices to direct costs) must be higher where the capital to labour ratio is higher, but net profits are influenced by monopoly power, the success of salesmanship and the luck of the game. Primary production, such as agriculture and mining, is strongly influenced by the vagaries of supply and demand and general swings of profitability with booms and slumps affect different markets differently. The concept of normal prices corresponding to a uniform rate of profit is only a preliminary step in the study of how actual prices behave.

Productive and unproductive labour. Marx took over from Adam Smith the distinction between productive and unproductive labour and gave it a different meaning. He distinguishes employment that gives rise to *surplus value* from that which does not. Thus industry and transport generate *surplus value* but commerce draws upon the surplus generated in industry. This does not mean that the expenses of handling, selling and advertising commodities are deducted from the profits of industry. Prices (relatively to money-wage rates) are set at a level that allows pro-

[8] See *Production of Commodities by Means of Commodities,* Part I, Cambridge University Press, 1960.

fits to be made in these activities and it is the consumers, that is the workers who have to cover the costs.

The distinction between productive and unproductive labour has sometimes been identified with the distinction between supplying goods and performing services. This has entered into the system of national income accounting used in the Soviet Union. There, final services are not included as part of the flow of production. In its context, this can be defended. It certainly does not mean that services are not important or that education and the armed forces are starved of funds. The purpose of national accounting in the Soviet sphere is mainly to record the overall growth of production. For the industrial sector, this can be shown in terms of physical output (though changes in composition and in quality are not easy to catch) but services have to be entered in the accounts merely as the salaries of those who perform them. However, this distinction between activities, such as transport, which contribute to physical output, and final services, which do not, is necessarily somewhat arbitrary.

The fact of the matter is that there is no perfectly satisfactory way of aggregating total production. Ricardo's search for an invariable measure of value was following a will-o'-the-wisp. The best way to organise whatever information is available is to treat it under two aspects. When we are thinking of welfare, we must consider the benefits derived from economic activity and then medical and educational services may be considered more valuable than most of the commodities sold in the shops. When we are considering distribution, we are concerned with flows of money payments and thus the division of proceeds between classes. Then the rate of exploitation, s/v, can be interpreted as the ratio of net profit to wages; $c + s$, corresponds to the flow of gross profits and v to the total wage bill.

Capital.   The rate of exploitation expresses the *share* of profits in proceeds. To find the *rate* of profit we must know the value of capital. In the formal model, Marx unfortunately uses the same symbols for flows as for stocks. He writes capital as $c + v$. To relate a flow to a stock we have to specify the turnover period. Let us take $c + v + s$ as the flow of *value* per annum. Then c is the depletion of the pre-existing stock of means of production that must be made good over a year. The total stock in existence, say C, is a multiple of this. (In a stationary state, C/c measures the average length of useful life of elements in the physical stock of capital.) Similarly, v is the wage bill for a year; in what sense is this part of the stock of capital? Marx describes it as *variable capital* and he regards it as that part of capital which is invested in employing labour and so generates *surplus value*.

For Ricardo, the wage fund was the main element in the stock of capital; it had a physical existence as a supply of corn in the barns after harvest which was to be paid out as wages, week by week, over the following year. Thus the wage fund required to employ a man was equal to one year's wage bill. In industry, a businessman has to pay out wages in advance of selling his product. For him, a wage fund is part of working capital. The relation of his wage bill to his wage fund depends on the short-period rate of turnover of his business. When he sells a batch of goods six months after work on them begins, his wage fund is half his annual wage bill; if eighteen months, it is one and a half times. For him, the wage fund is part of his invested capital on which he hopes to make profits along with the rest.

From the point of view of the economy as a whole, when production is proceeding smoothly, there is no meaning in a physical wage fund apart from the stock of means of production as a whole. The whole stock is being continuously consumed and replaced. When there is an unforeseen increase in employment, stocks are run down and shortages will appear of those which cannot quickly be replaced. Thus, the 'wage fund' in real terms depends upon the productive capacity of wage good industries (including agriculture). Thus it is necessary to re-interpret Marx's '*variable capital*'. The concept that only labour currently employed produces *value* must be related to v in its aspects as the wage bill. The whole flow of physical means of production used up over a year, including corn, should be represented by c, and the whole stock in existence by C. (On this view, the meaning of 'organic composition of capital' is the ratio of labour embodied in the stock of means of production to labour currently employed.)

In terms of a formal model, as Sraffa has shown, the complex of means of production corresponding to a particular technique, with a particular time-pattern of employment of labour in the maintenance of the stock, and a particular composition of output, can be represented in physical terms, while the level of prices, in any numeraire, real-wage rates and the rate of profit can vary to any extent with the rate of exploitation. This is the vindication of classical analysis as against the theory of marginal productivity of factors of production.

Technical change.   Marx's formal model is not well adapted to dealing with technical change. With a single technique (that is, the complex of methods in use for producing the whole flow of output of commodities) and a given composition of output, the relation of physical productivity to *value* remains constant as accumulation goes on and so do both the capital to labour ratio and the capital to output ratio (when the stock of means of production is valued in terms of the wage unit) for each department. Accumulation without technical change, however, can never occur. Economies of scale and new inventions are constantly changing the character of the stock of means of production and methods of deploying labour; the general effect is to bring about a continuous rise in the productivity of labour as capital accumulates (though changes in the design of commodities makes an exact measure of productivity unattainable). When physical product per man employed is rising through time, it is no longer useful to measure output in terms of *value*. Suppose that one million men are continuously employed, working an 8-hour day and 300 days per year; then the flow of *value* remains constant from year to year, however great the growth in the flow of commodities produced.

Marx was very well aware of this point. He describes capitalism as ripening the productive power of labour as though in a hot-house[9] but he was unable to fit this phenomenon into his formal model.

It is obvious that if the rate of exploitation remains constant while output per head is rising, the wage per man in terms of commodities is increasing as time goes by. (The growing alienation of mechanised work is another matter.)

The difficulty of conducting analysis in terms of *value* is illustrated by a curious error into which Marx fell in discussing the

[9] *Capital,* Vol. I, Chapter 25.

process of accumulation embodying technical progress.[10] He describes innovations in producing means of production which 'cheapen the ingredients of constant capital' and so tend to reduce organic composition (in modern terminology, the argument is that innovations may be capital saving), but he regarded this as an exceptional case. Normally, he maintained, technical change is accompanied by rising organic composition, that is to say that it requires an ever higher cost of investment per man employed. He points out that, if organic composition is rising and the rate of exploitation is constant, the rate of profit on capital must be falling. This is formally correct but irrelevant because it is unnatural to suppose that the rate of exploitation cannot accommodate to changing technical conditions.

A rise in organic composition means an increase in the capital to labour ratio. Since this comes about as the result of technical innovation, it will generally be accompanied by a rise in the output to capital ratio. A constant rate of profit then requires a rise in the real wage rate less than in proportion to the rise in output per head; that is to say, a constant rate of profit entails a rise in the rate of exploitation sufficient to offset the rise in the capital to labour ratio.

When innovations fail to raise the output to capital ratio, capitalists are not obliged to install them unless they raise profit per man employed at least as much as capital per man so that there is no reason to expect technical change, in itself, to cause a falling rate of profit.[11]

Depletion of resources. There is another problem which is of urgent importance today that cannot be well represented in terms of *value*. Marx assumes that the depletion of a pre-existing stock of means of production (represented by c) is continually made good by current labour. But some depletion, in particular that of minerals, can never be made good. The increase in productivity that comes about with technical change is very largely due to the use of energy to supplement human work. Mineral sources of energy – coal and oil – are now being used up in the industrial economies, socialist as well as capitalist, at a prodigious rate.

[10] *Capital,* Vol. III, Chapter 14.
[11] Cf. Joan Robinson, 'The Organic Composition of Capital', *Kyklos,* 1978.

Professor Reddy has pointed that, comparing countries, there is
a clear correlation between GNP *per capita* and the consumption
of energy per capita.[12] Public opinion in the wealthy countries
has begun to recognise that their life style and their technology
are excessively wasteful, though no one has much idea what to
do about it. For Third World countries to overcome poverty by
industrialising on the Western pattern is out of the question.
Certainly they need accumulation but they need to direct it into
forms suitable to their own situation.

[12] A. K. N. Reddy and K. K. Prasad, 'Technical Alternatives and the
Indian Energy Crisis', *Economic and Political Weekly* (Bombay), Special
Number, August 1977.

3

LAND AND LABOUR

The main influence upon the organisation of agriculture and the distribution of its products is the system of land tenure. Geography and climate are obviously of great importance, but different types of organisation can produce different consequences in the same natural conditions. Thus the productivity of agriculture is basically determined by the political and social setting in which it takes place.

There is a great variety of systems of land tenure amongst the countries of the Third World, some the legacy of colonialism, some inherited from ancient times though overlaid with Western systems of law and administration, some imposed by conquest in the past, some installed by recent revolutions and some evolving within the modern market economy.

The various types of system may be considered in terms of the manner in which a surplus is extracted from agriculture and the uses to which it is put.

Export economy

The intrusion of the capitalist economy into what is now the Third World began with trade in search of exotic commodities and went on to organise production of some of them on the spot. To set up a plantation requires land where soil and climate are propitious to the crop required say tea in the highlands of Ceylon (now Sri Lanka), sisal on the East African plateau or rubber in the jungles of Malaya, and a labour force to produce it. Under the European empires, grants of lands for capitalist investment were made available; a labour force had to be recruited from men and women whose need to earn money made them willing to accept strict discipline, low wages and in isolated life away from their home communities.

In South India, the system of land tenure had created a class of agricultural labourers, living wretchedly, tied by debt to a kind of serfdom. In the nineteenth century, they could be attracted to work on plantations in Ceylon and Malaya by the prospect of even the slightest improvement in their condition of life.

Within India, workers were recruited for tea and indigo plantations by providing loans which, at low wages, could never be paid off.

There was migration also from China into Malaya and Indonesia, and both Indians and Chinese were shipped to the Caribbean as indentured labour to supplement the work force provided by the descendants of imported slaves. The memory of the slave trade lies heavy on the conscience of the Western world but commercial substitutes for it are quite acceptable.

In Africa a system of taxation was introduced to generate a need to earn money, and cheap manufactured goods were dangled before the people in the interior so as to break up the self-sufficiency of tribal economies. Plantations in Africa generally employed a small group of permanent workers while the main labour force was composed of a revolving fund of migrants who came to earn the money they needed and then returned home to communities where they retained some rights to land. Food supplies for the plantation workers were drawn from purchases from the surrounding peasantry, so that the money economy spread out in an expanding circle.

The main overhead cost of a plantation was the expensive expatriate managers and plant for an elementary stage of processing the product. Investment mainly consisted of the initial waiting for the first generation of plants to come into bearing. Finance was therefore the principle requirement for the business, and reinvestment of gross profits from the plantations themselves provided for expansion when the market was expected to grow.

The plantation economy was devoted to export (though in India a market developed also for tea to be consumed locally) and its profitability varied with the state of demand relatively to supply in the Western economies. When demand was expanding ahead of supply the business was extremely profitable, both to producers and dealers. When the market was slack, part of the loss was passed down to the labour force by reducing employment and cutting wage rates.

The plantation economy certainly brought about a great increase in production (sometimes from land that was otherwise vacant) and it brought a great flow of money receipts to the colonial region, but the greater part of this was returned to the metropolitan country as profits, as savings of the expatriates and as demand for imports for them and for the small section of local society that grew up around the colonial administration. An enclave of Western business was developed in the colonies, oriented towards the economy of the metropolis, contributing little to the development of the rest of the territory except what was required for its own security and comfort.

In parts of Africa highly productive and profitable farms were established by Western settlers, introducing modern techniques while employing local labour at low wage rates. Here the most intractable of all the problems of the Third World remain to be disentangled.

Plantations (along with mines) are a legacy left to post-colonial nations but, as we shall see in a later chapter, it is not always easy for these countries to get command of the surplus that was formerly being extracted from them to use for their own purposes.

In Latin America agriculture was developed in the first instance to supply foodstuffs to the mines. The surplus was literally extracted from the ground, as gold and silver. Later an export economy was developed by local landowners and capitalists to supply sugar, coffee, wheat, meat, fruits and other products to the West. This surplus paid for the import of manufactures absorbed by the growth of a large urban middle class, with all the services that it required, including the apparatus of government and armed forces of the states concerned. It also paid tribute to British capitalists in the form of interest on loans but, before the great slump of the 1930s which destroyed their export earnings, very little of the surplus was devoted to investment in productive industry.

Landlords

Different types of agricultural organisation are seen where remnants of pre-colonial systems have survived into modern times. The period of colonial rule and the spread of the market economy have everywhere broken down and distorted ancient systems of land tenure and methods of extraction of a surplus (some of which were no less harsh than any now in force). But underneath modern commercial relationships, old traditions and old stratifications of wealth and power are still influencing the forms that underdevelopment and development are taking in agriculture today. In some regions, stagnation or sluggish growth prevails. In others, the introduction of modern agro-technology has raised productivity and is increasing the wealth of those who can take advantage of it, while often poverty is increasing for those who cannot.

One type of organisation is found where large proprietors (whether their title derives from ancient rights or modern purchase) get their holdings cultivated by tenants who have to pay them a share of gross product. In this system where the landlord (often an absentee) is content with his traditional income and status and does not aim to improve his estate, all the work and management is provided by the share-croppers (though in some countries, for instance Egypt, the national administration offers some control and assistance). The landlord has nothing to do but to extract his share of the gross product. The cultivator can grow only traditional crops by traditional techniques, and has too precarious a life to risk any experiments.[1]

The share in gross product taken by the landlord is generally set at some traditional level such as one half, but when population pressure has brought into being an indefinite number of would-be tenants, competition may shift the share to the advantage of the landlord. With any given share, the landlord gains more from his estate, up to a certain point, the larger the number of tenants he crowds on to it, that is, the smaller the holding granted to each

[1] Cf. W. Ladejinsky, 'Food Shortage in W. Bengal – Crisis or Chronic?' *World Development*, Feb. 1976; and 'Green Revolution in Bihar,' *Economic and Political Weekly*, 27 Sept. 1969.

share-cropper. The limit is set by the principle of diminishing returns. The amount of work per acre that a family puts in over the year is independent of the area of land that they have to cultivate, or even grows greater as the area grows less, in their desperate effort to live. The smaller the holding per family, the greater the amount of work put in per acre over the estate as a whole, and the greater the total gross output from which the landlord takes his share. The increment of gross output per acre grows less as work per acre increases until a point is reached at which the intensity of cultivation is so great that it is impossible, with the prevailing technique, to get any more out of the land. (This is a piece of classical economic theory which seems, by and large, to be borne out by experience.)

The tenant has to provide for the maintenance of working capital out of his share in gross output and often of some fixed capital as well (in India, bullocks and ploughs). Under some forms of tenancy arrangements, the landlord provides seed and other inputs (taking a larger share accordingly), but in any case the tenant has to feed his family from harvest to harvest. The smaller the size of his holding, the less his gross income, and the harder it is for him to maintain his working capital. When, owing to a bad crop or to family circumstances, he cannot live from his share in the last harvest until the next, he has to borrow. Then he must pay interest out of his share in the next harvest. Once in debt, he may never get free, for now he keeps a smaller share than before out of each harvest and is likely to have to borrow again.[2]

Over the seasons, there is generally a strong rise of prices, from the period of plenty after one harvest to the period of dearth before the next. The landlord and the money-lender claim payments immediately after the harvest; the cultivator's dues are reckoned (whether he pays in cash or in kind) at the moment when prices are lowest; when he has to borrow again, later in the season, they have gone up. It follows that, as well as rent and usury, the cultivators have also to cover the expenses and profits of the merchants who hold stocks which they cannot afford to keep themselves. In general, the smaller the cultivator's gross

[2] Cf. A. Bhaduri, 'Agricultural Backwardness and Semi-Feudalism', *Economic Journal*, March 1973.

income, the smaller the share of it that he can keep for himself.

In some regions the landlords maintain an attitude of feudal superiority and leave the business of money-lenders and merchants to a different class. In other regions, the moneyed interest has taken over the land so that rent, usury and dealer's profits are all combined in a single hand and the tenants are completely dependent on a single master.

In Latin America, what may be called commercialised feudalism, which was implanted by Spanish and Portuguese conquerors in the sixteenth and seventeenth centuries, survives today in some regions in the form of large estates – latifundia – inherited by a small number of families and cultivated (since slavery was abolished) by workers who are allowed small patches of land (minifundia) from which to feed their families.[3]

There are some wage earners but for the most part the labour force for the estates is provided by feudal types of tenancy in which rent is paid by working on the lord's land and providing various specified services. Holdings allowed to workers are kept small to prevent them from acquiring independence. Credit is provided by the landowner and is often managed in such a way as to create debt slavery. As with caste in Hindu societies, concepts of ethnic superiority, of blue blood over mestizo, and mestizo over Amerindians and blacks, give an extra sharp edge to exploitation.

In the nature of the case, large land holdings of this type are not propitious to technical development. The owner of a large estate can get a handsome income from a low level of production per acre, simply because he has a large number of acres. This system gives little incentive to landlords to increase productivity through investment and modernisation. Indeed, it is hostile to improvements that would raise the standard of life of the cultivators and make them less helpless.

It is sometimes said that the landlord–usurer squeezes his tenants too much for his own interests. If the cultivators were better fed, they could work harder and produce a larger gross output; but if the men had a higher net income, there would be less presure on the women and children to work. Under-nourishment shortens life, but this does not affect the landlord for there are

[3] Cf. D. Lehman, University of Cambridge Latin American Studies Working Paper, 1976.

always plenty of would-be tenants to replace those who are lost. Malthus maintained that there is a tendency for population to rise until the production of food per head is at the subsistence level. He forgot about rent and usury. Those who produce food eat only a fraction of it. Misery is experienced much before the intensity of cultivation is so great as to reduce total output per head to the subsistence level.

The general effect of the remnants of quasi-feudalism that remain in the Third World today is to retard both the growth of output and the development of a humane society. Total production and the transfer of product from agriculture to the rest of the economy are stagnant or grow very slowly. The spiral interaction of agriculture feeding industry and industry equipping agriculture fails to take off. Employment, which distributes claims upon a share of the product within agriculture, grows more slowly than the population. Redundant workers are expelled from the rural economy before industry has grown up to absorb them.

Peasantry

There are different systems, also inherited from the past, in which individual families or communities have rights in land, sometimes in difficult terrain where the power of landlords had not penetrated.

So long as a holding is large enough to support a family without an impossible level of toil, a system of peasant property is the most favourable for the cultivators, but it does not provide the basis for development of the economy as a whole. The independent peasant has neither the motive nor the means to produce much more than is required for the consumption of his own family. A peasant community with sufficient land can be almost entirely self-sufficient and has little need to trade with the urban economy, but the urban economy needs agricultural supplies. Urban civilisation has required to extract a surplus from agriculture by means of rent, taxation or labour services. Only when industry is already highly developed (as in modern Japan after an earlier history of severe exploitation) can the transfer of produce from agriculture be made by 'fair exchange' between the sectors of the economy.

Moreover, even for the peasantry, prosperity often destroys

itself by increasing numbers. Whatever system of inheritance
prevails, so long as rights in land are attached to the family,
growth in the size of families reduces land per head. In some
cases a family growing from generation to generation may continue to crowd on to the same holding. Most often holdings are
split up so that the area that the average cultivator works grows
smaller and smaller as time goes by. (In some parts of Ceylon,
fragmentation has gone so far that holdings have been split not
only in space but in time – various claimants take turns to cultivate
a few acres, season by season.[4])

As the land available to a family is reduced, they work harder
but beyond a certain point it is impossible to keep up their output.
Consumption falls and, in any emergency, many are reduced to
extreme misery.

Polarisation

Even when the overall ratio of labour power to land is fairly
constant, inequalities arise in a peasant community unless there
is some mechanism (as in many tribal societies or in the ancient
Russian *mir*) to redistribute land amongst families periodically.

Differences in luck or diligence, and in the accidents of family
life, bring about differences in the relation of consumption to
production for various individuals. When commercial, monetised
relations prevail, those who are obliged to consume more than
they produce get into debt or lease out land to others. Those who
have a margin over consumption add to their income out of
interest and rent.

When this inherent tendency to polarisation within a commercialised peasant community is combined with growing pressure of population, it works all the faster.

There is some evidence that, in certain regions of the Indian
subcontinent, a surplus of manpower in relation to cultivable land
first emerged in the second half of the nineteenth century.[5] There
began a drift of the less fortunate families into a deficit position
which obliged them to borrow in order to live. Money-lenders

[4] See B. H. Farmer, *Pioneer Peasant Colonisation in Ceylon,* Royal Institute of International Affairs, 1957, p. 57.
[5] See P. Sanghvi, *Surplus Manpower in Agricultural and Economic
Development,* Asia Publishing House, 1969.

and merchants found a profitable outlet for finance in supplying the deficit, and acquiring property for, as the burden of debt piled up, a family were finally obliged to part with their land.

Thus, from generation to generation, the total production of the less fortunate families was insufficient to provide their minimum consumption and the deficit was made up by gradually dissipating the capital wealth represented by their rights in land. The process could be long drawn out, for the pressure of demand was at the same time raising the value of land, so that the borrowing power of a family did not fall as fast as the size of its holding.

Savings out of the income from rent and usury were mainly devoted to acquiring land, by purchase or through forclosing unpaid debt. These savings were thus devoted to making up the deficit in the consumption of the poor peasants rather than to financing investment in improving the productivity of agriculture or supplying means of production to industry.

Any peasant family that could keep its head above water could improve its position by renting in land and employing wage workers to cultivate it, or buying up land and leasing it out.

The combination of growth of numbers with the monetisation of traditional relationships produces complicated patterns of leasing and sub-leasing and of taking or giving employment. Old families break up and new ones prosper. Sometimes the same household is both renting in land from other owners and renting out part of their own. Sometimes a man whose main livelihood is earned from wages also has to employ a worker on a scrap of land that he still holds because his duty to his own employer prevents him from finding time to cultivate it in the rush season. A family that has too little land to be able to live may lease it out to a prosperous neighbour, so that the landlord is poorer than the tenant.

A family which already owns some land can lease in more while one which has too little to occupy its labour power has not sufficient credit to be able to acquire more. Those whose need is most desperate find it hardest to get loans. The distribution of land within a peasant population follows the rule: to him that hath shall be given and from him that hath not shall be taken away.

The results of the operation of this rule are illustrated in independent India. The census of 1971–72 showed that 60 per cent of rural households were poor peasants with too little land to be able to survive from its produce, operating 9 per cent of the area of cultivable land, while 10 per cent were well-to-do farmers cultivating 53 per cent of the area. The poor peasants often lacked equipment, even ploughs and draught animals, which they were obliged to hire. The well-to-do farmers had the lion's share of cooperative credit and of irrigation facilities. They had the further advantage that they could produce the most remunerative crops, while the poor tenants were struggling mainly to feed themselves.

The intermediate group, 30 per cent of all households, were classed as small farmers operating 38 per cent of the area. Of these families, at any moment, a few might be managing to climb up to the condition of well-to-do farmers and many were on the slippery slope down to landlessness.

The situation varies in different parts of India. In Kerala, for instance, only 1 per cent of rural households cultivate more than 10 acres (the holding of a well-to-do farmer), while in Rajasthan, 78 per cent of the area is cultivated by 33 per cent of all households, enjoying the status of well-to-do farmers (many are raising livestock). Between these extremes, other districts lie around the average.[6]

Every peasant society has its own character, often with roots in a long past history, and none can claim to be typical, but nearly everywhere the same principles are at work. The extreme misery of some is an opportunity for gain to others. The hard struggle for existence obliges the peasants to exploit each other. There may be societies in remote regions that maintain traditions of a different way of life, but it seems that all are being more and more sucked into the market economy.

Distribution of holdings

An unequal distribution of land entails an unequal distribution of food. In the agricultural sector of most of the Third World, over the last ten or fifteen years, there has been an appreciable

[6] See Dalip S. Swamy, 'Differentiation of Peasantry in India', *Economic and Political Weekly*, 11 December, 1976.

increase in output and in income per capita, but at the same time an increase in absolute poverty, in the sense of the proportion of the rural population living on a diet below what is considered locally to be the minimum of subsistence, an increase in the proportion of landless workers and a fall in the level of their real earnings. This has been carefully documented for seven Asian regions (including the prosperous Indian Punjab). The eighth, Bangladesh, is exceptional in that there overall per capita income has been falling, but there also inequality has been increasing.[7]

For India as a whole, the same dismal picture is reflected in official statistics :

The proportion of India's population living in abject poverty, as measured by the officially recognised norm of monthly per capita private consumption of Rupees 20 at 1960–61 prices, is significantly higher now than it was a few years ago. According to a Government of India estimate, two-thirds of the people in India now live in abject poverty, as against 45.6 per cent in 1964–65. In other words, the number of people living in abject poverty went up from 218.20 million in 1964–65 to 387.47 million at the beginning of the country's Fifth Five Year Plan (April 1, 1974).[8]

The growth of poverty is often attributed to the growth of population; certainly the absolute numbers of miserable people would have been less if the total population had been smaller, but since per capita GNP has been rising and so has per capita consumption of food, inequality of distribution is the main cause of the existence of large numbers of people who are unable to satisfy the need for even a minimum standard of nourishment.

Quite apart from its influence upon welfare, the inequality of the size of holdings has an important technological aspect. An unequal distribution of land tends to reduce the total productivity of a given amount of effort. Here again the principle of diminishing marginal productivity applies in reality in a rough and ready way. The intensity of cultivation on small holdings is greater than on large.

Where a family cultivates their own holding, all work and all share in net income. Their motivation is to carry the intensity of cultivation to the point where an addition to annual output, due

[7] See Keith Griffin and Azizur Rahman Khan, 'Poverty and Landlessness in Rural Asia', mimeo, ILO, Geneva, 1977.
[8] Anand P. Gupta, 'Solving India's Employment Problem', ILO, 1975, WEP 2–33/WP 28.

to harder work, is not worth the extra effort. The smaller their holding, the lower the income for the family, the more important is every mouthful and the greater the effort that it is worth while to make. In the limit, they are obliged to push the intensity of cultivation to the point where doing more work would not increase the product at all (the point where the marginal productivity of labour is zero).

On a large holding, where net income is relatively high, the family does less work (womenfolk stay indoors and the children go to town to school) and cultivation is largely by hired labour. The principle of diminishing returns then indicates that it pays to employ workers up to the point where the additional product of an additional unit of labour time covers the addition to the wage bill, plus the extra nuisance of organising and supervising the work. (That is, where the marginal product is not less than marginal cost.)

Where the proportion of landless men and very poor peasants in the rural population is large, the wage rate may be very low, but the cost to the family of employing outside labour is always greater than of using their own. Thus the intensity of cultivation is generally less, where wage labour is employed, than on small family holdings. In reality of course, calculations are not made so precisely as in an economics textbook, but the general principle is found to be broadly true in practice.

Furthermore, on large holdings land may be used in such a way as to save labour and other inputs. Thus longer fallows reduce the need for application of manure or artificial fertilisers and pastures save stall feeding of cattle.

Thus it is generally found to be true that, for a given area of land, with a given potential labour force, total output is greater the more equally holdings are distributed.[9]

The drawback of small holdings is that each family has to produce a range of products, so that it is not possible to bring about the specialisation of land to its best uses. The Chinese system of large communes divided into small teams combines the advantages of intensive use of labour (now being gradually equipped with machines) with control over the use of land in

[9] R. Albert Berry and William R. Cline, *Farm Size, Factor Productivity and Technical Change in Developing countries*, mimeo, World Bank, 1976.

large units. It has the further advantage that team members have a strong motive to put in extra work to improve their land in schemes which can be organised on an appropriate scale. The team as a whole, in effect, owns the land and any improvement in it increases both individual and collective income for the future.

A number of attempts in various countries have been made to regulate the distribution of land holdings or to protect the interests of tenants by legislation; many have failed to make much improvement in the situation of the poorest cultivators and some have made it worse. Well-meaning legislation is frustrated by the weakness of the officers charged with its administration in face of the power of wealth in the rural community. Often peasants refuse to accept their legal rights for fear that the 'big men' will take revenge on them later. Sometimes a reform in tenant rights brings the main benefit to well-to-do farmers who have leased in land from the poorest.

A ceiling on the size of permitted holdings has led to land-owning families sharing out titles to their whole estate amongst themselves, leaving no land to be distributed to tenants. In West Bengal, we are told, cynicism has reached such a pitch, that the name of a horse may be accepted for a share in an estate where, presumably, there were not enough cousins to go round.

When some land from large estates is distributed, a cruel conflict of interest is created between those who have become smallholders and those who can no longer find employment for wages.

To give titles to land without adequate provision for credit is a mockery. Sometimes rights to purchase have been taken up by the rural moneyed class (usurers and merchants) who become even more exacting to their tenants than the old-style landlords, or from fortunes made in business, now escaping taxation or turning 'black money into white'. The attempt to give security of tenure by giving a permanent claim on land that has been cultivated for three years running, causes landlords to shift tenants round every two years.

Schemes to supply credit and organise supplies and marketing credit through local cooperatives, and technical assistance of various kinds, have had some successes here and there, but in general they are found to play into the hands of those who are already better off and to increase inequality within rural communities rather than to reduce it.

In general the benefits of reform have been found to accrue to the most prosperous elements of the rural population and they have generally acquired sufficient political influence (whether under dictatorship or in nominal democracy) to see that changes that threaten their interests are frustrated.

The land reforms in Egypt, carried out in 1952 and 1961, were conceived as a revolutionary attack on feudalism. A large amount of land from the states of the exiled Turkish nobility was available for distribution and a ceiling was fixed on local landholding. The reform was less ineffective than most because a special administration was charged with the provision of credit, collection of dues and dissemination of technical advice so as to protect the interests of the poor peasants and to help them to increase their productivity. Over the years, however, this system has been swamped by the growth of population and the spiralling influence of differential rates of accumulation. Now the distribution of holdings is no less unequal and the proportion of landless families no smaller than anywhere in Asia.[10]

In Latin America, in general, reforming governments are not permitted to survive for long; the military regime in Peru set up by the coup of 1969 was somewhat of an exception (though a shift to the Right occurred in 1976). There, a scheme of land reform was initiated by expropriating large estates and turning them over to cooperatives of tenants and workers. In principle, these should become the property of the cooperatives, but meanwhile the appointment of managers and provisions for credit and marketing are turning them into a kind of commercial farm employing wage labour. It has turned the peasants into a proletariat. This makes business-like organisation possible and leads to improvements in methods of production and provides a surplus to support industrialisation. Thus land reform, intended to save the peasants from exploitation, has been turned into a more efficient, because less brutal, method of exploiting them.

[10] See M. Abdel-Fadil, *Development, Income Distribution and Social Change in Rural Egypt 1952–1970*, CUP, 1975.

Modernisation

A special kind of modernisation of agriculture has developed from within peasant communities of which the most famous example is in the Punjab in India.[11]

Even when inputs other than work come into operation it is still found to be true that output per acre tends to be higher the more equally ownership of land is distributed (allowing for differences in terrain), but the difference is less marked than with traditional techniques.[12] The higher the income per family, the greater is the possibility of employing labour to improve the land and of increasing investment per acre, in working capital such as fertilisers or fixed capital such as pumps and machinery. Moreover, a large holding makes it possible to experiment on part of the area with new techniques or new varieties of seed and then to expand the use of those that prove successful. The innovations that go under the name of Green Revolution have increased the return on investment in agriculture and so enhanced the advantages of the richer over the poorer cultivators, though not enough to compensate for the greater intensity of the application of labour to land.

In districts propitious to modernisation, that is where irrigation is available, a new class has emerged of rich peasants who have consolidated holdings large enough to make investment profitable. In the process, small holders have been squeezed out and tenants dismissed. The rich peasant has a surplus over the needs of consumption which he can plough back into investment to increase his surplus in the future. Moreover, he can borrow on better terms than his poor neighbours. It pays him to borrow so long as the value of increased yield, say from using more fertiliser, is greater than the interest charge – a different matter from borrowing in order to remain alive. He may also be able to hold back sales until the market is favourable instead of having to part with his crops just when prices are lowest. (In some districts, including the Punjab, there are organised markets, with floor and ceiling

[11] Cf. W. Ladejinsky, 'Green Revolution in Punjab', *Economic and Political Weekly*, 28 June, 1969.
[12] Berry and Cline, *op. cit.*

C

prices, but the level of prices is set to suit the interests of the rich peasants.) Thus the rule that to him that hath shall be given works all the faster when modernisation is going on.

The rich-peasant economy is a form of incipient capitalism but it seems to have narrow limits. The same family system exists as among smallholders; after a certain level of prosperity has been reached in one generation, the next generation often splits up holdings into smaller units.[13] A great deal of investment goes into house building and when wives are kept at home they have to be given spending money to amuse them, which is a drain upon the reinvestment of profits into the land.

Moreover, the profit to be gained by investment in improving productivity has to compete with the return of rent in leasing out land and interest on money lending. It requires a large technological jump (such as the Green Revolution) to make it worth while. When the possibilities of a jump have been exhausted, small piecemeal improvements may not provide sufficient attraction to keep investment going.[14]

However, this system has advanced far enough to bring into operation a new type of agricultural organisation. Investment and improved techniques have increased the flow of output from a given area of land. The consolidation of holdings has reduced the number of self-employed cultivators and increased the hiring of wage workers. The net effect upon the overall ratio of labour to land may go either way.

Innovations can be roughly divided into those which are primarily land saving (that is, increasing output per acre) and those which primarily save labour by reducing work per unit of output.[15] The use of fertiliser and high-yielding seed is mainly land saving. The use of tractors is an intermediate case. It substitutes a few skilled drivers for armies of workers, especially in harvesting, but at the same time it releases land required for the keep for bullocks, it improves ploughing, and by speeding up the cycle of processes it sometimes makes multiple cropping possible,

[13] See S. Bhalla. 'New Relations of Production in Haryana Agriculture', *Economic and Political Weekly Review of Agriculture,* March 1976.

[14] See Utsa Patnaik, 'Class Differentiation within the Peasantry', *Economic and Political Weekly Review of Agriculture,* September 1976.

[15] See C. H. H. Rao, *Technological Change and Distribution of Gains in Indian Agriculture,* Institute of Economic Growth, Delhi, 1975.

which could not be fitted into the growing season with slower labour-intensive methods of cultivation. The extreme form of labour saving equipment is represented by the combine harvester.

It seems that, on the whole, higher yields per acre increase employment up to a certain point because of the larger quantities of crops to be handled and then prevent it from expanding further. In any case, wage rates are kept low. The demand for labour is largely seasonal and may be met by migrants from poorer districts. If a scarcity of labour did develop, it could be countered by further labour-saving mechanisation.

The tenant or smallholder is idle in the slack season but he does not think of himself as unemployed; the income of his family is earned over the year and is eked out over the year, not divided into a period when it is possible to earn something and periods when it is not. Moreover, a claim on the smallest scrap of land gives a sense of security and self-respect which the mere wage earner has lost. The rich peasant economy, where it flourishes, increases national income and provides for the transfer of agricultural output to the rest of the economy, but from the point of view of the rural population as a whole it is not much of an improvement on the old system of extracting rent, usury and trading profits from the production of the self-employed cultivator.

The quasi-feudal agriculture of Latin America, from the first, had some characteristics of capitalism, extracting profit from commercial sales. Now it has had modern capitalism thrust upon it from without. Corporations, mainly financed from the USA, have taken over great tracts of land for agribusinesses supplying commodities such as beef, fruit and cotton partly to national urban centres but mostly to the United States. These find it profitable to use highly mechanised and land-extensive techniques, reducing the opportunities for the local population either to feed itself or find employment for wages.

The most notorious case is that of Guatemala. After a reforming government was thrown out, as is now acknowledged, through the machinations of the CIA, the authority of American corporations, including United Fruit, was firmly re-established. Almost all fertile land is in their hands and a large part is kept empty while the peasants live precariously in the mountains, so as to prevent them from establishing an independent economy of their own.[16]

Another type of case developed in Mexico; northern deserts, otherwise useless, were irrigated and a labour force recruited to cultivate cotton and the new 'miracle' strains of grain. These developments gave Mexico for some years a record rate of growth of agricultural output which, however, left the mass of the rural population quite untouched.[17]

Capitalist agribusiness is the most powerful instrument for extracting surplus from the land, but the surplus is not mainly put at the disposal of the regions where it arises. The essential mode of operation of this type of organisation is to carry supplies away from the under-nourished populations and provide them to those who are already over-fed.

Capitalist farming, whether of the rich-peasant type or of the great agribusiness, modernises production and increases output; it makes investment in improving the land and provides the surplus potentially available for the development of industry. At the same time it deprives growing numbers of access to the land and increases the polarisation between wealth and misery.

Only in China has a system been evolved which permits the cultivators to benefit themselves while supplying the needs of the economy. Land reform was a great political upheaval that freed the peasantry from the psychological as well as the economic oppression of landlords. Even before the recent growth of numbers, the ratio of labour to cultivable land, in China, was the highest in Asia. After the distribution, holdings were so small that it was easier than in other socialist countries to persuade the peasants of the advantages of cooperation. Groups of workers, in teams or brigades within the wider organisation of Communes, are now for the most part cultivating the same land on which their ancestors grew up. Individual work of men and women is rewarded by shares in the income of the group, and collective work, on schemes of irrigation, terracing hillsides and so forth, is rewarded by improved productivity for the future. Study and experiment, as well as scientific advice, diffuse technological pro-

[16] R. H. Chilcote and J. C. Edelstein (ed.), *Latin America: The Struggle with Dependency and beyond,* Chapter 1.
[17] *Ibid.,* Chapter 2.

gress. The present drive for mechanisation is aimed at increasing output while reducing the burden of toil. It does not displace families from the land, for any labour time that is saved can be organised in small-scale industries on the spot. This system combines the advantages of self-employment by the cultivator on his own land with the advantages of large-scale management and the promotion of investment.

The transfer of agricultural produce to the rest of the economy is organised by a system of quotas for deliveries, paid for at fixed prices, which is designed to skim off the excess of production over local needs. Communes which enjoy the most favourable natural conditions have the largest quotas and the highest money incomes. Their members can enjoy a better standard of life than those of poorer Communes, while at the same time carrying out more investment to increase their differential advantage in the future. A problem thus emerges for the authorities of how to check the growth of inequality without interfering with the growth of productivity. However, a floor has been set under the standard of life everywhere, so that this kind of inequality is not so distressing as inequality between those families that have something to eat and those whose have not.

4

TRADE IN PRIMARY COMMODITIES

The Third-World countries of today were drawn into the capitalist world market, under regimes of formal and informal colonialism, as appendages of the metropolitan nations to supply raw materials and exotic commodities to the industrial centre. These may be divided into broad types, though there are important variations within each type. Minerals had to be produced where the deposits were found. Animal products required vacant land for ranching. The tropical belt around the world provided facilities for vegetable products, some, such as rubber, transplanted from west to east; some, such as coffee, from east to west. These provide the basis for consumption-goods industries, especially some fruits, tea, coffee and chocolate, and for some industrial raw materials including rubber and natural fibres. They now provide the basis for export earnings which are potentially valuable for development, but their distribution amongst the territories of modern states is completely arbitrary, depending upon accidents of economic geography and of their history in colonial and neo-colonial times.

This raises once more the question of what constitutes a national economic entity. The sources of raw materials which were developed by investment from the metropolitan countries are largely still owned and controlled by capitalist corporations. Mining companies in Africa, for instance, employ local labour and have been induced to train local personnel for the lower rungs of management but policy is still in the hands of the overseas headquarters and is administered on the spot by expatriates whose loyalty is to the corporation rather than to the country where they are working. The policy is directed towards making profits for the corporation as a whole. When a single corporation operates in many countries and in many activities – for instance fabricating metal as well as mining ore, the amount of profit attributable to any one activity can be manipulated, by the prices at which products are transferred from one branch to another, to suit the convenience of the corporation, not the needs of the country where the activity is carried out.[1]

The share in proceeds that the local government obtains as royalties and taxes depends upon the relative economic power and negotiating ability of the parties when an agreement between the corporation and a newly-independent government was drawn up.

One of the most recent examples, iron mines in Mauretania, is one of the most striking, because the country where the investment was made was almost completely non-developed, being inhabited mainly by nomadic herdsmen. The mines were opened up by foreign capital, a railway and a town were built to service them. Many of the workers recruited for the period of heavy investment were unable to return to their old life when it was completed and now hang around as urban unemployed. The mining company was highly successful; exports and statistical GNP rose rapidly. The higher salaried staff are expatriates. The local economy, in 1970, received less than 20 per cent of gross proceeds from the current wage bill and payments to the state.[2]

In several cases a small country has become dependent upon the resources for a single product (such as copper mines in Zambia) which are exploited by capitalist corporations, so that national income and government revenue are largely determined by the terms that they choose to offer.

There is nothing in economic theory to say what is a fair return on natural resources. A corporation can claim that a country within whose boundaries ore happens to have been discovered had neither the finance nor the know-how to develop for itself. Only investment and management by the corporation have turned it into economic wealth. The spokesman for the country can reply that without access to its soil no wealth could have been created. Here there is a sharp clash of interests which cannot be settled by appeal to any accepted rules.

[1] Cf. S. Lall, 'Transfer Pricing by Multinational Manufacturing Firms', *Oxford University Bulletin of Economic and Statistics,* August 1973.

[2] Samir Amin, *Neo Colonialism in West Africa,* Penguin, 1973, a translation of *L'Afrique de l'ouest bloqué,* Hogner, 1971.

To keep up supplies to the industrialised countries will require new investments, and the Third World countries may be able to demand stiffer terms in the future. Then the interests of the industrial nations will be involved and the outcome will depend upon the balance of power in the world market, not upon any economic principle.

For plantations, investment is less important and know-how easier to master. The main advantage of expatriate management is in general business sense, in the power to discipline labour and in trade connections. The government of Ceylon (now Sri Lanka) for long after independence hesitated to nationalise the tea gardens, while talking about doing so, for fear that their own people would not be able to run them efficiently. Meanwhile the owners naturally extracted as much of their capital as they could by not re-investing amortisation funds in replanting and general maintenance, so that the productive capacity of the plantations was impaired by the time that they were finally handed over.

Another type of export business, which brought more benefit to the local economy, was the purchase from peasant producers, by dealers, for instance of groundnuts from Senegal and cocoa from Ghana. The West Coast of Africa, up till the second world war, was protected by the mosquito from expatriate settlements. The producers were self-employed and managed their own business. A surplus was extracted from them mainly in the form of dealers' profits.[3]

There are also a number of crops for export produced by small holders side by side with plantations – for instance, bananas, coconuts, coffee and some tea. An important example is that of rubber in Malaysia, where, as well as large estates, there are small family holdings and intermediate-sized holdings worked by share-croppers. The intensity of application of labour is generally greatest on the smallest holdings.

So long as peasants retain enough land to feed themselves, the supply of the cash crop is elastic; when price falls, less is marketed, and families can continue to live; but where the lure of a cash crop has reduced food production, peasants become dependent on the market, gaining from high world prices and suffering extremely from low.

[3] See Polly Hill, *The Gold Coast Cocoa Farmers,* Oxford, 1966.

In early days of rubber production in Malaya, the small-holders were found to be more efficient producers than the large estates and the British administration put obstacles in their way, to favour the planters.[4] More recently, the benefit of research and development carried out for the estates has been shared with the smallholders.

Large estates (whether capitalist or cooperative) have an advantage in dealing with perennials – trees or bushes – that have to be renewed at intervals, since a part of the area can be replanted while production continues from the rest. This is an offset to the intensity of small-scale cultivation.

Where an export crop is purchased by traders from small-holders, a marketing board, such as Ghana and Nigeria inherited from the British administration, is a partial substitute for nation-alisation. The Cocoa Marketing Board arranges purchases from scattered producers, brings the cocoa beans down to the ports and fixes a price which is intended to be kept fairly stable at a level which will attract supplies. The prices received for exports fluctuate around a level above the procurement price, thus the government receives a part of the surplus generated by produc-tion. However, when it comes to settling the export price, the marketing boards are in a weak position in confrontation with the bargaining power of the two or three transnational corpora-tions who are the only buyers; in effect, their dependence upon foreign capitalists is hardly less than that of the countries which have been obliged to allow their mineral resources to be developed for them.

Commodity prices

The export earnings a country can get from its primary resources (irrespective of who enjoys the revenue) largely depends upon the prices of the particular commodities it has to sell. There are general swings up and down of primary prices relatively to manufactures with world booms and slumps. There are move-ments relatively to the general level for particular commodities and particular countries experience different results from offering

---

[4] See P. Bauer, *The Rubber Industry,* Chapter. 24 §15, London School of Economics, Longmans Green, 1940.

the same commodity. The pattern of prices in world markets at any moment and its evolution through time are extremely complex and any general observations about them are necessarily over-simplified.

Even as a simplification, the labour theory of *value* is not much help in this context. When qualitative differences in products are due to natural conditions there does not seem to be much advantage in comparing one with another purely in terms of *value*, that is, labour embodied. We may say: 'A man's a man for a' that' and an hour of work anywhere in the world creates an hour of *value* but that is a moral statement not an analytical proposition.

There is no point in trying to define a unit of *abstract labour* to apply over the whole world. There are problems even within one capitalist economy of the proper weighting, for instance, of skilled and professional work in terms of a unit of 'ordinary' labour; when the difference between one kind of production and another is strongly influenced by natural conditions it is impossible to give such weighting any practical meaning.

Moreover an analysis in terms of *value* requires the means of production to be measured by labour embodied. This may be applicable to industrial plant, but not to natural resources. In opening a mine or a plantation, some investment of finance creates a large block of natural wealth, of which the earning power thereafter depends mainly upon market demand for its specific product. The flow of *surplus value* accruing to its owners must be regarded as rent rather than profits; the long run tendency to equalise the rate of profit on investments of this sort is very weak. (The financial value of such an asset is reckoned as the flow of net receipts discounted at the appropriate rate of interest, so that commercial success or failure appear as capital gains or losses.)

Installations such as mines and plantations were set up by profit-seeking investment, and in that respect they are no different from industrial equipment, but once they are in operation, they yield rent to their owners. The contribution that they make to current output does not bear any regular relation to the value of the labour embodied in them when the initial investment was made; moreover the return that they yield varies with the prices of the particular commodities that can be produced by labour working with them, and it may be much greater or much less, from time to time, than a normal rate of profit on the investment.

Thus, neither *values* nor 'prices of production' provide a useful approach to relative prices of primary commodities. Timeless general equilibrium has no application here, but there is something to be learned from Marshall's treatment of supply and demand for commodities 'one at a time'. All prices interact with each other, but it is legitimate to isolate special factors which affect particular commodities. Marshall took the example of fish.[5] Here we may illustrate the analysis in terms of a tree crop, say cocoa. In a given short-period situation, there is a certain productive capacity in existence, that is, a number of bushes in bearing. As with Ricardo's corn, there are differences in productivity of work applied to different stands because of differences in yield or in location in relation to transport. Thus we can make use of Marshall's construction of a short-period supply curve. For each quantity of output (in the season) there is a certain *supply price* which just covers its *cost at the margin* so that a further increment of output would add more to costs than to receipts. A rise in demand from one season to the next pushes out the margin, raises the price and leads to an increase in output. (Marshall considers also the reaction of a higher price on demand, but here the proximate demand comes from dealers; we will discuss their reactions below.)

In any actual case, there are many complications to be brought into the argument. For instance, when the producers are independent peasants, there is an element of 'effort demand for income' to be considered. In some situations, a rise in price may reduce output because the need for extra money has become less urgent. The elasticity of supply of the cash crop is also influenced by the alternatives available, in particular for growing food for home consumption. For plantations, the cost of additional finance may be an element in supply price. Every type of case has its own detailed characteristics, but the broad principle of rising short-period supply price generally holds.

To continue the Marshallian story; supposing that the high demand continues to rule, the producers are enjoying high

[5] See *Principles,* 8th edition, p. 369 et seq.

returns. This leads to an expansion of capacity – more planting, postponement of scrapping old bushes and so forth. Prosperity continues until the new capacity comes into bearing. Then supply increases beyond its former maximum and the price begins to fall.

Marshall implies that profitability falls back to some 'normal' level but in this type of case new investment generally overshoots the increase in demand that brought it about. A period of low profits discourages maintenance (say, replanting of tree crops) so that when demand expands further, a shortage appears. Thus particular commodities experience cycles of their own, independently of general booms and slumps.

Marshall also discusses the relations of demand to supply in the case of joint products, of which there are many examples among natural commodities. Before the advent of refrigeration, beef in Argentina was a superfluous by-product of the trade in hides; afterwards the position was reversed. In the short-run, a rise in demand for wool leads to an increase in flocks of sheep and makes lamb more plentiful, but in the longer run it causes merinos to displace crossbreds and reduces the supply of meat. The coconut palm provides many examples. Husks from which the fibre, coir, is extracted are a by-product of copra. Toddy and copra are rival uses of the palm, for one that is tapped for liquor yields fewer nuts. And so forth. This whole field of inquiry has fallen out of fashion since 'microeconomics' was taken over by general equilibrium. To understand the behaviour of relative prices of commodities requires a great deal of historical and analytical study of particular cases.

There are also important macroeconomic implications of relative movements of demand and supply, as we shall see below.

Terms of trade

There has been much discussion of the overall terms of trade between primary and manufactured products and much complaint from spokesmen for the Third World that the world market system operates unfavourably for them.

We can get some light on this question by first considering the mechanism of international price formation as it works out in competition between the Western countries. The main influence on relative prices of industrial products is the movement of money-wage rates in terms of world currency (US dollars when the dollar was supreme) relatively to the relative growth of productivity. Where output per head is rising faster in one country than others, due to technical innovations, superior skill and discipline of the labour force, capital accumulation and economies of scale, the fall in relative costs tends to be offset by a correspondingly faster rate of rise of money-wage rates. Where the offset is not complete, the country concerned is a low-cost producer; it has a competitive advantage over its trading partners and enjoys an increasing export surplus. Thus, to be a low-cost producer is highly advantageous.

When the competitive advantage of one country becomes an embarrassment to the other trading nations, it may be obliged to appreciate its exchange rate. A rise in the exchange rate makes home produced goods more expensive to foreigners, just as does a rise of money-wage rates, thus it puts a drag on competitive advantage, but it has been found in recent years that the exchange rate mechanism is not strong enough to offset deep-seated differences among capitalist economies.

In the Third World countries, the level of wages on plantations and mines is kept low by a massive reserve of unemployed labour and the absence of strong trade unions. Where comparable commodities are produced in the West as well as in the Third World (say, sugar in Australia) output per head is generally much lower in the Third World (because of the high investment that has taken place in the West) but wage rates are lower in a greater proportion, so that the Third World countries are low-cost producers. Does this give them an advantage in trade?

Where there is direct competition between natural commodities and synthetics performing the same function – for instance fibres and rubber – low wages have proved an advantage in a defensive sense, for if costs had been higher those products might have been wiped out altogether. In many lines, however, while it is true that the lowest-cost producer has a competitive advantage, this is only an advantage over other producers of the same commodity. For all of them together, demand at any moment is rigid and does not vary much with prices. One can take the market away from another and so appear to gain from being able to sell at a lower price, but the total demand for the commodity as a whole is not increased.

Competition between rival producers, say of tea or oil seeds, may shift demand from one to another but it does not bring about an increase in total receipts for all the competitors taken together. Indeed, when demand is 'inelastic' to price, a reduction in selling price increases the amount bought, if at all, less than in proportion to the fall in price, so that total receipts for all the sellers of the commodity taken together are reduced. This situation is sadly common in the market for primary commodities.

For this reason, the favourite remedy of the IMF for a trade deficit – depreciation of the exchange rate – is often disastrous. Devaluation by a country which is an important source for a commodity precipitates a fall in its price and reduces export earnings all round.

Many countries, each anxious for exports, can produce the same or closely similar commodities; they keep prices low for each other by causing supply to run ahead of demand. Thus, the entry of East Africa into the production of tea and coffee has been a disadvantage to India and Brazil. All three southern continents compete with each other in many tropical specialities. Each can gain an advantage in competition with the others but the result is to keep down the gains from trade for the Third World as a whole.

The main cause of the historical rise of real wages in the West has been the accumulation of capital relatively to the growth of the labour force, and technical innovations increasing productivity interacting with a strong labour movement – rising output per head making wage demands possible and wage demands promoting labour-saving innovations.

Among animal and vegetable products, there have been some notable achievements of scientific research and development such as the famous high-yielding varieties of wheat and rice and improved clones of rubber but engineering provides more scope than biology for continuous progress. Moreover, where progress has taken place the benefit has gone to landowners and capitalist producers rather than to wage earners.

In the prevailing conditions of under-employment, for instance in India, mechanisation of production and transport increases misery. In the production of coir in Kerala – disagreeable work at much less than a living wage – a simple mechanical device would have reduced employment by a third and, with the same price of the product, offered double the wage rate. The workers prevailed on the State government to prohibit its introduction. By contrast, in a self-managing cooperative, such as a brigade in a Chinese commune, scientific and mechanical progress is eagerly pursued for the benefit of all the members as well as of the national economy.

Certainly, it is true that there is unequal exchange of Marxian *values* in the sense that the purchasing power of an average hour's labour over commodities of all kinds is far higher in the industrial centre than in the primary-producing periphery, but behind this lies the economic and social history of the last three hundred years. Since the Third World takes part in the world market system, it is entangled in the conditions that the system imposes.

Monopsony

Unfavourable terms of trade emerge in a more or less competitive world market; they are also influenced by the inequality of the commercial and financial power of the parties concerned.

Even in competitive conditions, there is a large gap between the sales value of a raw material at the point of export and at its final destination, which covers transport and handling costs and the profits of dealers. Freight rates are kept at a level that makes shipping profitable. For the workers employed in transport and commerce, wage rates are generally much higher than those in the producing country, and dealers' profits have to be high enough to cover the risks (from their point of view) created by fluctuating prices. Furthermore, nowadays the world market is far from competitive. For most raw materials, the fabricators have open or tacit cartel arrangements to limit competition amongst themselves, while they are buying from weak, scattered and competitive sellers.

The trade in tropical foodstuffs has been to a large extent

taken over by a few large transnational corporations, who evidently do not compete keenly with each other but agree in keeping down purchase prices.

This phenomenon is strikingly illustrated by the trade in bananas. Two corporations, with another smaller one, dominate sales in USA, West Europe and Japan, and dominate purchasing in the producing countries, particularly in Central America. The formation of a union of banana exporting countries (UBEC) precipitated a trade war in 1974 in which the buyers penalised countries which tried to impose an export tax by refusing to buy, stopping production on their plantations, and physically destroying boxes of bananas at the ports. The buyers won, and the taxes were withdrawn.

The break-down of the final price in 1971 was such that the gross return to growers was 11.5 per cent of proceeds. The retailers' gross margin was 31.9 per cent. The rest was costs and profits on transport and handling. Formerly shipping and ripening were provided by separate companies. Now the great corporations are integrating these stages of the business, presumably saving costs and increasing their own profit margins.

Technical changes, such as disease resistant breeds, irrigation and improvements in packing and transport have lowered costs. The benefit was partially passed on to consumers but not at all to the primary producers.

The inability of countries competing with each other for exports to restrict supply has led to a continuous deterioration of the terms of trade for the sellers of bananas.[6]

The corporations pass a part of the surplus that they extract from the Third World to the rich countries in taxation (though they are experts at evasion), to rentiers, and in the salaries of their personnel (some of whom may be nationals of poor countries by origin); the rest they amass as finance to increase their own operations.

The consumers in the rich countries have the advantage of secure supplies and guaranteed quality, as well as of the low cost at point of origin (though this makes only a small difference to the final price). It is in this sense that workers in the rich coun-

[6] See F. F. Clairmonte, 'The banana empire', CERES, FAO, Jan/Feb. 1975.

tries, as well as capitalists, are benefiting from the exploitation of the poor countries.

This story is typical of many food products supplied to Western consumers by the great monopsonistic buyers from the Third World.

Instability

The greatest drawback of depending upon primary commodities for export earnings is the unpredictability of the market. The agricultural sector within an industrial economy usually has enough political leverage to see that it is sheltered in one way or another from the worst effects of instability, while strong capitalist firms in extractive industries can form protective rings for themselves. The Third World countries which import such commodities must pay the protected prices, while their own products, for the most part, are left to the mercy of the laws of supply and demand.

Instability is at three levels. For particular commodities, changes in technology, in consumers' habits or in prices of complementary or substitutable commodities, from time to time cause unforeseeable long-run changes in conditions of demand. These may go either way; for instance, the demand for natural fibres was first devastated by synthetics and then revived by the rise in price of oil that made them expensive. As the rich countries grow, demand sometimes runs ahead of potential supply, so that one commodity or another enjoys a seller's market for a time. This very fact encourages both substitution and a search for new sources of supply so that the advantage of scarcity is soon lost. There is likely to be a general long-run tendency to check the growth of demand relatively to supply; the great versatility of modern technology and the malleability of consumption at a high standard of life mean that no individual natural commodities are indispensable. In spite of all the anxiety nowadays about exhaustible resources, it seems likely that the central buyer will continue to have the whip hand over the peripheral seller for a long time still.

Changes on the side of production also create instability. Crop failure in one region gives a sudden bonus to rival producers in others, or the opening up of a new source of supply is a disaster for the old ones.

Such accidents affect particular commodities. General and chronic instability is transmitted to the market as a whole from the instability of the industrial capitalist economy. The rise and fall of activity in booms and slumps at the centre affects all the countries of the periphery, and the ebb and flow of military expenditure affects very many.

On top of the large swings in demand are superimposed continuous day-to-day oscillations in prices. Direct purchase by the great corporations bypasses the organised produce exchanges, but they still have an important sphere of operation in the trade in many commodities. The business of dealers is to bridge the gap both in time and space between producers and purchasers. They invest finance in buying commodities from the original producers and pass them on to the buyers as required.

The opportunity to make profits by this use of finance arises from the shortage of finance that usually besets the sellers, particularly of seasonal crops. The working capital of a producer is absorbed in a season's output and he needs to sell in order to replenish it and start the next cycle of production. The dealer can buy when price is at its lowest, hold stocks and feed supplies out to the market as prices rise. The inability of the producers to hold back sales to wait for a rise of price is most pronounced for small peasants, but even institutions such as a marketing board may be pressed for cash. Moreover, to hold stocks is to take a risk. Apart from more or less predictable seasonal swings, movements in commodity prices are continually being brought about by changes in the relations of supply and demand. The dealers have to be better informed about market conditions than the producers and, indeed, part of their business is to make profits out of superior knowledge and successful guess-work.

This business is necessarily speculative in the sense that it depends upon taking a view of what will happen next. According to textbook theory, dealers perform a service to the economy by buying in stocks when prices are tending to fall and selling out when prices are tending to rise, thus stabilising prices through time. But guess-work is not always stabilising. Since each watches the others to try to divine how their guesses are going, there is a natural tendency for movements of opinion to set up perverse reactions. A rise in price, instead of restraining demand, as in the textbook theory, increases buying in expectation of a further rise and a fall in price increases sales. Thus, the dealers may themselves bring about the fluctuations that it is supposed to be their function to mitigate.

In popular language 'speculation' is a bad word, and certainly vicious manipulations of the market do occur, but in the general way this kind of speculation cannot be regarded as vicious for it is a normal and inevitable result of playing the game according to the rules of the free market system.

These three layers of instability – long-run shifts in demand, cyclical swings and speculative oscillations interact with each other, and for countries which depend on the world market for their export earnings, make coherent economic policy difficult and turn long-range planning into a dubious gamble.

Stabilisation schemes

The unsatisfactory operation of the market for commodities has long been recognised and spokesmen for the Third World are now urgently demanding reform. They hope to find means, within the world market system, to improve their terms of trade, and to mitigate the nuisance of instability, which works against their interests far more than in their favour.

In principle, the price of a commodity can be kept within a certain range by holding supplies off the market when demand is falling and releasing them when it is rising. This can be done through the operation of a buffer stock, buying and selling the commodity, or by an agreement among producers to restrict output when price has reached a lower limit and to permit sales to expand when price reaches an upper limit; or by some combination of these two principles.

There has been a great deal of talk about the advantages of schemes to stabilise prices but in practice very little has been done. At the time of the fourth UNCTAD Conference in 1976 there were only three schemes in operation, for tin, cocoa, and coffee.[7] 'The negotiation of even the successful agreements took

---

[7] UNCTAD IV TD 183, para. 49.

many years of tortuous and frustrating effort. The International Cocoa Agreement, for instance, took 17 years to materialise.'[8] This arises from the fact that the main advantage of stabilisation is to the sellers, who are weak and disorganised, while finance and economic power belong to the buyers – traders and manufacturers in the industrial countries.

The instability of primary product prices is a nuisance for buyers as well as for sellers, but the problem is much more urgent for the sellers than for the buyers. The cost of materials plays a small part in the total trade of the industrialised economies and a still smaller part in their total income, while for many Third World countries receipts from sales of a single commodity, or two or three, dominate their export earnings, and export earnings have a strong influence over the prosperity of their whole economy. From a national point of view, the rise of prices is far less damaging to the buyers than a fall to the sellers, while from the point of view of the traders and manufacturers concerned, in the industrial country, most of a rise in costs is passed on in prices to their own customers. The buyers, therefore, have much less at stake than the sellers. Moreover, the ideology of a capitalist democracy permits government interference with the free play of market forces to favour interests in the home country (for instance by support prices or protection) but is extremely reluctant to admit any responsibility for the effects of home policies upon interests abroad.

If the problem were merely fluctuations of prices about a predictable trend, the operation of a buffer stock would clearly be profitable and capitalist finance would be devoted to stabilisation. But a trend is something that statisticians can perceive over a run of years in the past. It cannot be perceived in advance, particularly in the present age of drastic political and technological discontinuities in the evolution of patterns of supply and demand.

[8] An international Cocoa Agreement was finally ratified in 1972. This was based upon the principle of a buffer stock designed to maintain prices within an agreed range, supplemented by a system of quotas to regulate supply. It has not yet been proved in action because market prices have been consistently above the specified ceiling since it was set up. The range of prices was raised three years after the agreement came into force, but it has not yet been effective. See Tetteh A. Kofi, 'The International Cocoa Agreement' *Cocoa Production, Economic and Botanical Perspectives,* John Simmons (ed.), Praeger, 1976.

The buyers have generally found that a period of scarcity and high prices for a particular raw material leads before long to a shift in demand (say, the substitution of a synthetic for a natural product) and calls into being fresh sources of supply, so that a brief seller's market is followed by a prolonged buyer's market. (This is just what the spokesmen for the sellers complain of.) The free market system hitherto has suited the interests of the buyers on the whole and they do not encourage plans to interfere with it.

On the side of the sellers, there is a general interest in stabilisation and improvement in their terms of trade, but there are conflicts of interest amongst themselves. The basic mechanism of stabilisation is to withold supplies from a falling market, but for any one seller it is better to get something than nothing. There is always a temptation to sell, although at the expense of another supplier's market, and the temptation is all the stronger when a scheme to raise prices is getting under way. Restriction requires the imposition of discipline over individual interests in a common cause. This means that there must be an authority in each country where the commodity is produced to regulate output, for instance by a system of central procurement or by the allocation of quotas; there must be an agreement amongst the countries on the distribution of the burden amongst them and there must be mutual confidence that it is being fairly carried out.

Furthermore, there are great technical difficulties in arriving at an agreed formula for dealing, for instance, with the relative prices of varieties and grades, for what goes under the name of any single commodity is by no means homogeneous, either technically or commercially. A scheme which has to cover a number of sources of supply involves conflicts of interest amongst them; there is a general conflict between new entrants to the market who want to be allowed to expand their share in output and the old producers who want to restrict it; and there are innumerable minor conflicts over details in any scheme, which make it hard to find a formula which all parties will, first, agree to accept and, second, abide by in face of change. When the buyers are not particularly keen on supporting an agreement, they have ample opportunity to play upon the conflicts within the group of sellers.

Over and above all these difficulties, the sellers lack the finance required to set a scheme afloat.

In 1974, the General Assembly of the United Nations issued
a declaration on the establishment of a New International
Economic Order, in which an important element was the need
for a reorganisation of international trade in a manner less unfavourable to the interests of Third World exporters. At the
fourth UNCTAD Conference in 1976, proposals were put forward for an integrated programme for regulating trade in ten
principal commodities. (These are coffee, cocoa and tea, sugar,
cotton, rubber, jute and sisal, and copper and tin.) In spite of
many political and commercial differences of interests amongst
themselves, the Third World countries at the conference presented
a united front in their demands upon the industrial powers, but
the latter were very reluctant to grant their case. In the end it
was conceded that a fund should be set up to be used in some
still undetermined way to assist in regulating trade and there was
a promise of further discussions about the problems presented by
the chosen commodities. So long as the laws of the market prevail, a weak seller cannot gain an advantage over a strong buyer
merely by passing resolutions in however august an Assembly.

Monopoly power

There is one notable case in which a group of sellers were able
to use the laws of the market in their own favour – that is the
rise in the price of oil in 1973. The Organisation of the Petroleum
Exporting Countries was founded in 1960. It arose out of con-
versations between Venezuela and Iran with the Arab League
about the possibility of defending the oil exporters against reduc-
tions in the price being imposed upon them by the international
oil companies. A secretariat was set up, and all the exporters
made gains from their improved bargaining position.[9]

For the Arab League, oil had always had a strategic and
political importance. In support of the October War with Israel
in 1973, a boycott was instituted against Israel, the USA and
Holland. (The distributing companies went through the motions
of implementing it while seeing that none of their customers were
effectively deprived of supplies.)

[9] See Zuhayr Mikdashi, *The Community of Oil Exporting Countries*, Allen
& Unwin, 1972.

This experience made the Arabs realise the potential monopoly power of the oil producers and OPEC imposed a quadrupled price of oil. This was implemented by the distributors, who made enormous profits for themselves.

The success of OPEC has inspired the idea that other groups – for instance, the sellers of bauxite[10] – might also exercise monopoly power to improve their proceeds from sales, but it is unlikely that any general solution to the problem of the weakness of Third World exports could be reached by this means.

There were certain unique features about the case of oil. First, the whole pattern of development in industry had grown round cheap oil from the Middle East, so that demand was inelastic and could not quickly be shifted; secondly, the main producers were bound together by a political motive and had no difficulty in carrying the smaller ones with them; thirdly, the largest producers were in the unusual position of having a sparse population (as well as preserving a highly unequal distribution of income) so that the only imports they required were luxury goods, prestigious buildings and armaments. They had no urgent need for any more export earnings than they were receiving already, and so they did not have the usual reluctance to restrict output in order to maintain the level of prices for the group as a whole. Finally, the distributors were ready to play along with the producers, and, indeed, made huge profits for themselves in the process. This concatenation of circumstances is unlikely to be repeated.

The spokesmen for the industrialised nations appeared to be deeply shocked by the whole affair, but, though OPEC states regard themselves, formally, as part of the Third World, it is only natural that their sudden wealth should incline them towards playing the financial game according to the rich countries' rules.

World inflation

One of the complaints made by spokesmen for the Third World is that the purchasing power of their exports is constantly being eroded by inflation in the industrial countries raising the prices of the products that they want to buy.

[10] Cf. C. F. Bergsten, 'A New OPEC in Bauxite', *Challenge*, July/August 1976.

In the capitalist world today, there are two separate systems of price formation, which can be broadly distinguished, though there is some overlap between them.

For primary products, as we have seen, prices oscillate with the relations of demand to supply; for manufactures, a system of cost-plus prevails; that is to say that the businesses concerned form selling prices by adding a gross margin to direct running costs (wages, materials and power) calculated to cover overhead costs at some normal level of operation, plus an allowance for net profit.

There are great differences in the power of different types of business to control the prices at which they sell, but monopoly does not necessarily mean restricting output to keep profits high, for the great corporations compete with each other, continually expanding into new markets. The general rule that movements of prices are governed by movements of costs applies to them as much as to small competitive producers.

The main element in costs in industry as a whole is the cost of labour. The price level for manufactures in general is therefore governed by the relation of money-wage rates to productivity. The level of wage rates, in turn, is determined by the fortunes of the class war, that is the struggle of organised labour to maintain its share in the proceeds of industry.

During the long run of expansion and prosperity (interrupted only by minor recessions) for a quarter of a century after the end of the second world war, real-wage rates were rising in all the Western countries, though, as we have seen, their fortunes were not all alike. The continuous rise of money wage rates, necessary to keep the share of real wages from falling, had a tendency to overshoot, so that money wages rose faster than productivity, bringing about a rise in the level of prices; thus, what now seems a mild degree of inflation became chronic.

During this period, various commodities experienced different movements but, on the whole, growth of supply kept ahead of demand and the terms of trade, overall, moved in favour of manufactures.[11] This contributed to the rise of real-wage rates and to some extent to allay inflation in the Western countries. But foodgrains were an exception. The growth of prosperity, par-

[11] UNCTAD IV ID 184, Supplement 4, Chapter 1.

ticularly in the Soviet sphere, was increasing the consumption of meat and deflecting grain into feeding livestock.

In the 1970s a strong boom developed, particularly in the United States, and the prices of materials shot up. The rise in the price of oil in 1973 exaggerated a movement that was already taking place. In industry, a rise in the cost of materials raises prices relatively to money-wage rates, and therefore generates a demand for a compensating rise in money wages.

Thus the Western world experienced an alarming increase in the rate of inflation, which coincided with a serious slump in activity; the slump brought a fall in the prices of industrial materials (except for oil) but inflation in the West continued and, with rising unemployment, the class struggle became all the more embittered. This experience has brought about a new phase in capitalist development. Western governments are now more anxious to check inflation than to preserve employment. (The neo-neoclassical economists have obligingly come forward with a new theory that inflation is due to a decline in unemployment below its 'natural level'.)[12]

Now as soon as an upswing in industrial activity causes material prices to begin to rise, fear of inflation puts a brake on revival. The new international economic order which is evolving in this situation does not seem to be propitious to meeting the demands of the Third World to an improvement in their share in the benefits of international trade.

Self-reliance

In the United Nations, the people of each country are necessarily represented by its government. Arguments are conducted in terms of the level of GNP *per capita* and its rate of growth, and in terms of national advantage from trade. In all this, the declared objectives of development seem to be lost to view.

The underlying problem of hunger and malnutrition, even famine, of unemployment and underemployment, of rural poverty and urban degradation, are even more pressing today than they were a quarter of a century ago at the beginning of the phase of rapid economic expansion in the developed countries.

[12] Cf. Francis Cripps, 'Money supply, wages and inflation', *Cambridge Journal of Economics*, March 1977.

The fact that the developing countries did not share adequately in the prosperity of the developed countries when the latter were experiencing remarkably rapid expansion indicates the existence of basic weaknesses in the mechanism which links the economies of the two groups of countries.[13]

This is certainly true. The mechanisms which linked the economies of the periphery to the centres of capitalism in the colonial era have not been radically changed. But it is not only a weakness in external international relationships which prevents these problems from being solved. A government which was resolutely mounting a 'frontal attack on mass poverty and employment' would get a great deal of help from an improvement in its country's export earnings, which could be used to finance investment in improving the productivity of agriculture and increasing capacity to produce necessary consumption goods, but it is also true that an increase in the proceeds of foreign trade, in itself, cannot be relied upon to bring about an improvement in livelihood for the mass of the population. It may only increase economic disparities and aggravate social tensions.[14]

[13] UNCTAD IV TD 183, paras. 12 and 13.
[14] UNCTAD IV TD 183. See above p. 7.

5

AID AND LOANS

The confusion in orthodox economic theory between capital as financial property and as a functioning stock of means of production has bedevilled the discussion of development. For a long time it was the generally received view that poor countries are poor because they lack capital; for more than twenty years, the rich countries have been transferring capital to them through grants and loans; if the results so far are disappointing it is because too little capital has been transferred.

Gradually, experience has led to a more sophisticated interpretation of this process but the basic idea remains that the rich countries have already done a great deal to provide capital to the Third World and that they ought to do more. What is being transferred, however, is not a stock of means of production but *finance*, that is allocations of foreign exchange. Whether or not this is turned into capital in the sense of productive capacity depends on how it is used.

Here we will first provide a general account of the meaning of finance in order to try to dispel the aura of mystery that hangs about it.

Money and finance

An economy of any degree of complexity requires money, an abstract representation of purchasing power in which transactions can be conducted. Money is whatever is acceptable for discharge of obligations between members of the society concerned; the official money of a government is made acceptable by being 'legal tender' for the discharge of debts within the nation.

In a modern economy, a large part of the stock of money consists of bank deposits owned by individuals or institutions, which they hold as a store of wealth in a liquid form, so that they can draw upon it to make payments as required.

The purchasing power of a unit of national money over goods and services at home is the inverse of the level of prices. Its purchasing power outside is influenced by its rates of exchange with other currencies. (Great confusion in the international monetary system at the present time, with all exchange rates at the mercy of speculative movements, arises because there is no currency that is universally acceptable, as sterling was before 1914 or the US dollar between 1945 and 1971.)

For an individual, or an institution such as a business firm, to make payments in excess of current receipts requires an expenditure of *finance*. Payments may be financed by spending sums of money that the economic unit concerned already owned (say, in a bank account), by selling out some realisable assets that it held (say, gilt-edged securities) or by borrowing.

The most usual way for a business to finance investment is in the first instance to borrow from a bank and, when the venture has been successful in increasing its earnings, to issue shares or bonds and pay off the bank loan, thus renewing its credit for borrowing again. When a more or less constant proportion of investment is financed in this way, a higher rate of investment leads to an increase of bank lending. Expenditure from an increase in bank advances leads to an increase in deposits by recipients of these payments and so entails an increase in the quantity of money, thus providing the medium of exchange required for the higher national income that accompanies a higher level of investment.

Borrowing power is limited by the confidence that lenders have that repayment with interest will be made, and this, in general, is limited by the assets that the borrower can pledge as security. (In oriental societies, a great deal of even the most sophisticated modern business is run on a family basis. A ring of mutually supporting concerns often includes a bank which helps to finance the rest.)

For a national government as well as a business, expenditure in excess of revenue, a budget deficit, has to be financed by borrowing and the terms on which a government can borrow depend on its credit. When a government borrows by selling bonds to its own citizens, it places an obligation upon future tax-payers to provide for interest payments. (It is sometimes maintained that a national debt is no real burden on the economy because those who receive interest and those who pay taxes are all citizens of the same country, but raising taxation is a nuisance and there is a social cost, for only the wealthier citizens are able to buy bonds, while taxes fall upon everyone, including the poorest.)

Where a modern financial system has been established, part of the government's debt consists of the stock of cash in circulation. A currency note is, in essence, a government bond that carries no interest. People are willing to accept 'paper money' because of its convenience as a medium of exchange. At any moment there is a certain outstanding quantity of notes being held by individuals and institutions or passing from hand to hand in the channels of exchange.

When commercial relationships are gradually invading formerly self-sufficient villages, the need for currency increases and more notes will be issued, giving the government a painless way of supplementing its revenue.

As total national income increases, with a given pattern of habits of payments (the 'velocity of circulation of money'), there is a certain growth of the total stock of money that is required by the public. When the government and the banking system prevent the stock of money from increasing fast enough, finance is restricted, rates of interest rise and investment of all kinds is checked; when the quantity of money increases relatively to requirements, credit is easy and borrowing is stimulated.

Any expenditure of finance over and above current receipts represents an increase in the general level of effective money demand and when there is not a sufficient increase in the supply of output to meet it, there is a tendency for prices of commodities to be pushed up. So far as the primary effect of an increase in demand is concerned, there is no difference between an increase in a government's budget deficit and an expenditure of finance by private business but when a government covers its deficit, not by selling bonds to the public but by obliging banks to lend to it, there is a secondary effect of increasing the quantity of money ahead of requirements for it, and so making credit easy. This may

stimulate investment and speculation in the private sector, enhancing the primary inflationary effect of the deficit.

Once inflation has set in, with continuously rising prices, more
and more money is required, but then the government's expenses
are going up, and its credit may be impaired so that it cannot
sell bonds on reasonable terms and is obliged to borrow through
the banking system all the more.

The historical association of great inflations (such as that in
Germany in 1921–23) with a budget deficit that cannot be
covered by long-term borrowing has led to the view that 'using
the printing press' is the main cause of inflation, rather than a
symptom of it.

An alternative means of dealing with a budget deficit is for
a government to borrow from abroad instead of from its own
subjects. It can then sell foreign exchange to its citizens, which
they are very glad to be able to buy, and so collect the home
currency to cover its expenditure.

This solves its problem for the moment, but this is far worse
than borrowing by selling bonds to its own people. That lays
upon its citizens, for the future, the nuisance cost and mal-
distributional effects of raising taxation to pay interest to each
other. Over and above this, a foreign debt lays a burden upon the
country's balance of payments; over the future, it will have to
achieve a sufficient surplus of exports to provide for the service
of the debt.

Many of the successor governments of ex-colonial territories,
now part of the Third World, had a weak command over their
new fiscal system and used a large part of the loans offered to
them as 'aid' simply to cover their expenditures; they were, in
effect, borrowing from abroad to run budget deficits.

When a deficit was incurred for 'unproductive' uses – general
administration and the armed forces – foreign debt piled up without any corresponding assets being acquired. Insofar as government outlay is upon well-planned schemes of investment, say a
dam providing irrigation and power, there is, after some delay,
an increase in national output, but this does not guarantee a
sufficient increase in tax revenue, in terms of home currency, to
correspond to the service of the debt; and even if it did, there is
no guarantee that it would provide an increase in foreign earnings

(by raising exports or cutting imports) sufficient to implement the required payment in internationally acceptable currency.

Developing the New World

The notion of 'transfer of capital' promoting development is based on a false analogy with nineteenth-century experience; for instance it is said that the railways of North America or of the Argentine were 'built by British capital'. This appearance arose in special historical circumstances. On the one side were still untapped natural resources, a growing labour force and nations endowed with capitalist institutions and ideologies, offering dazzling prospects of profit to investors, but lacking developed financial structures, and not yet provided with all-round manufacturing industry; on the other side were a sophisticated capital market and available industrial productive capacity. It was easy to borrow by selling bonds in London; while the finance was being invested there was a strong demand both for means of production (steel rails, for instance) and for consumption goods on which growing profits and a growing wage bill could be spent. Since Britain was the main source of supply, the investment of finance generated a flow of exports for the country from which loans came, as well as an import surplus for the borrower. There is no reason to expect an exact correspondence between the flow of finance and the flow of trade but they told in the same direction. Both were consequences of a common cause – high investment overseas. Interest charges mounted up, but at the same time sources of supply of exports were being created, so that the return flow of financial payments was associated with appropriate flows of trade. Thus high investment in the borrowing countries generated an export surplus for the lender while it was going on; later the fruits of the investment produced an export surplus for the borrower, while growing income in the lending country generated demand for imports and there was no obstacle to repayment.

British finance, certainly, facilitated the spread of capitalism and the emergence of new groups of capitalists, but 'capital' in the sense of stocks of means of production embodying industrial technology had to be created by schemes of investment organised on the spot. There is no magic in 'importing capital' that can be relied upon to generate development unless the digestive mechanism of the recipient is able to make use of it.

Forms of aid

There are three main types of financial inflows to Third World countries – commercial loans and direct investment by private business (now coming mainly from the transnational corporations), payments earmarked for military purposes and allocations of finance provided by governments or international institutions such as the World Bank. The first two items will be discussed later; here we are concerned with the third. Part of this finance is 'aid' in the sense that it is a free gift; most is in the form of loans or guarantees of payments to private traders, offered on terms of interest and repayment easier in various degree than those required in the open market.

When aid is given for a particular project – say a dam, an iron and steel works or a luxury hotel to attract tourists – it comes in a package with technical assistance and organisation. The concept of 'importing capital' then, on the surface, seems quite plausible; the new installations are there for all to see. The benefit to the receiving country depends, obviously, on the appropriateness of the new equipment to its needs, and the extent to which its own technicians and workers are able to operate it. India and Brazil could digest an iron and steel industry, whatever use was made of it later, while some small countries have been led to accept projects more useful to the donor's economy than to their own.

A case in point was the Volta River project. The Volta dam in Ghana was undertaken with a view to supplying electricity for the production of aluminium. The dam, the power station and port facilities were paid for half and half by the Ghana Government and the World Bank. An aluminium refinery was set up by an American company, Valco; bauxite is brought in, and aluminium exported again. The government made a bad bargain, as they undertook to supply power to Valco at cost. The proceeds are hardly more than sufficient to service the debt. The power is managed by Ghanaian personnel and there is an ample supply of electricity, some of which is sold to neighbour states. Apart from this, Ghana gains nothing from the project, while Valco gains a great deal.

Some of the most acceptable aid comes from the small Nordic countries which have no obvious political axe to grind and send advisers who make an intelligent and sympathetic analysis of local requirements and possibilities.

Even when aid is bound up with technical assistance, it is still misleading to call it a transfer of capital. It is primarily a supply of foreign exchange. Part is earmarked to pay for the services of expatriate advisers and for imports of ingredients to go into the installations being set up; the rest is exchanged for local currency to pay local costs and so becomes available for other overseas payments. Moreover, a particular project may be a substitute for something that would have to be done in any case and so releases foreign exchange for other uses.[1]

The difference between aid tied to projects and a supply of disposable finance is partly a matter of degree. Guarantees are usually attached to particular suppliers and even general loans are usually accompanied by advice and criticism; whatever the advice may be worth, the main point of aid is the provision of foreign exchange that permits the country to meet a deficit in its balance of payments.

The foreign payments that a country has to make arise partly from financial obligations – to permit repatriation of profits by foreign businesses or to meet interest charges on former loans – and partly from the cost of imports. The services which loans are performing for a country is thus to enable it temporarily to avoid bankruptcy and to purchase more imports of goods and services than would otherwise be possible. Contributions that it makes to development depend on what form the imports take.

In official language, imports are described as 'real resources'. In the philosophy of the free market economy, imports are justified by the fact that they meet demand from individuals, businesses and institutions that have money to pay for them. Meeting demand is by no means the same thing as contributing to development. From the point of view of the market, money is money

---

[1] Cf. M. Kalecki and I. Sachs, 'Forms of Foreign Aid' in *Essays on Developing Counties,* Harvester Press, 1976.

D

whoever spends it, for whatever purpose, but from the point of view of development, there is a great deal of difference between one kind of demand and another. Debt which is incurred in importing luxury goods is inimical to development, first because it is wasting foreign exchange that might be used to contribute to productive investment; secondly, because it provides a model for a type of consumption which will attract home resources, so that import-saving investment is deflected from the lines of production required to meet more important needs; thirdly, because it is directing demand away from generating employment of labour at home; and fourthly because it leaves behind a burden of debt against which there is no corresponding asset.

To confine imports to what is most useful for development would require a strenuous social and political policy to prevent luxury consumption, a high degree of control over the economy and a well-conceived programme of investment to make sure that imported commodities and services are used to the best advantage. A country which tried to embark on such a policy is unlikely to receive aid from the West. In the philosophy of the aid givers, laisser faire and free trade were the road to prosperity; conditions attached to grants of aid were designed to head off any attempts to deviate from it. Moreover, it was convenient for the donor countries that demand generated by aid should be for commodities that they could profitably supply.

An important benefit to be expected by donor countries from aid lay in an increase of exports while the finance was being spent. According to proper free trade principles, the recipients of loans should have been free to spend the finance wherever they found the market most favourable, so that the various industrial countries would have to compete with each other for orders. This principle was not maintained for long. In the early years after the war, the position of the United States, both as a source of finance and as a source of importable goods, was even more completely dominant than that of Great Britain had been in the nineteenth century. Funds provided in dollars were automatically spent in the USA. Later, the recovery of European and Japanese industry raised competition for American exporters; dollar loans began to be used to discharge debt to third countries. Consequently, rules were introduced which ensured that dollar finance could be used only for payments in the USA. The other countries followed suit by tying whatever aid each gave to its own market.

An incidental effect of tying aid was to reduce its purchasing power to the recipients. Exporters in the donor country, having a captive market, were able to raise prices for the goods they supplied above the level ruling where competition obtained.[2] The recipients were unable to complain, for if they did not receive tied aid, they would receive none.

A special form of aid in the immediate post-war period consisted in the export of American grain under Public Law 480. A system of price support maintaining the internal terms of trade for agriculture led to the accumulation of stocks of grain in the USA. At the time of acute scarcity of dollars after the war, it was impossible to find overseas buyers; an ingenious scheme was devised which made it possible to give the grain to countries in the Third World in return for a deposit of counterpart funds in their own currencies, to be used by the US authorities for local expenses. P.L.480 was passed in 1954 in order to permit the US authorities to undertake these transactions. The cost of the food to the recipients consisted of the inflow of dollars that they would otherwise have received from American expenditure in the countries concerned.

The availability of imported grain permitted the authorities in the recipient countries to postpone the political and economic reorganisation of agriculture that would have been necessary to make them self-sufficient. It is a matter of dispute whether, in the long run, it did more harm than good to the recipients.[3]

Mercantilism

For a planned economy, economic philosophy is quite different from that of the capitalist world. The benefit derived from trade consists in imports, which supplement home production, while exports are a cost, depleting home consumption. (In some cases,

---

[2] Cf. E. Eshag, 'The Cost of Aid-Tying to Recipient Countries', Progress Report by UNCTAD Secretariat, TD/71, 8 September, 1965.

[3] Cf. Raj Krishna, 'Government Operation in Foodgrains', *Economic and Political Weekly*, 15 September, 1967.

there are exportable products which are surplus to home requirements, but even they have some cost in terms of labour and
transport facilities.) When a country's resources are already fully
employed, an increased export surplus can come about only at
the expense of consumption or investment at home. In such a
case, giving aid is properly described as a burden. Aid, of course,
is given primarily from political motives both by planned and
capitalist governments, but in so far as repayment is required,
socialist donors ask for it in terms of imports of particular commodities. These are a benefit to consumers in the donor countries
in a straight-forward sense, while repayment may be an indirect
benefit even to the debtor, by leading to employment of labour
that would otherwise have been idle and developing resources and
trade connections which will later become export earners. (In
India, however, there are complaints that erratic bulk purchases
by the USSR destabilise the market for some agricultural
specialities.)

In the free market sphere, exports are desired, by capitalists
and workers alike, as a source of profits and employment while
imports (except for raw materials unobtainable at home) represent undesirable competition. A private enterprise economy
suffers from a greater or less deficiency of effective demand, apart
from rare moments of strong boom. A seller's market, in which
demand is beating against the limit of productive capacity, cannot last long, for it leads to investment and recruitment of labour
to increase capacity; this is liable to over-shoot, causing a buyer's
market to supervene. For any capitalist country, at any moment,
profits and employment would be higher if only exports were
greater. (The transnational corporations have developed pat-
riotism only for capitalism as such and do not recognise any
distinction between home and foreign production, but for the
rest of business and for the whole labour force, the economy of
my country is still a matter of paramount importance.) Trading
nations have always been mercantilist at heart. To establish a
case for adopting free-trade policies it is necessary to argue that
the advantage to the country's exporters of eliminating protection
abroad is a more than adequate *quid pro quo* for avoiding protection at home.

The advantage, for a national economy, of what is called a

favourable balance of trade, that is an excess of exports over imports, as the original Mercantilist economists saw,[4] lies in the immediate stimulus that it gives to activity at home – providing opportunities for making profits and organising employment in excess of those offered by the home market – which is quite apart from any long-run gains that may accrue from amassing claims to repayment.

Donor governments, however, like to proclaim themselves to be carrying a burden in a good cause, and they are liable to be reproached by voters at home: why are you giving money away when so many of our own people are in want? At the same time, they do not think it proper to depart too far from the usual rules of free-market economic relationships. It seems natural to give aid mainly in the form of loans, with conditions of repayment attached, as though it were of the same nature as the nineteenth-century flow of finance for profit-seeking investment, which was expected to bring a return to the lender. However, the donor countries were not at all keen on developing an import surplus which would make repayment possible. To make service and repayment of loans possible, the donor countries would have to develop a surplus of imports from the debtors but this was not to their taste. Until OPEC took the law into its own hands, industrial countries did very little to support schemes designed to improve the terms of trade for primary products; the system of tariffs inhibited processing of raw materials on the spot, which would have made it possible to export them with a higher value; manufactured exports from the Third World were narrowly restricted.

The paradox of aid, when the mercantilist spirit dominates the world market, is that the donors benefit from what they give away and then demand repayment which they do not want to receive. However, as we shall see, they had other ways of using the system to their advantage.

Creditors and debtors

Illusions about the meaning of a transfer of capital were even

---

[4] Cf. J. M. Keynes, *General Theory,* p. 355 et seq.

more prevalent amongst the recipients than amongst the donors. When talk about development began to be fashionable, most of the Third World countries were in possession of reserves of foreign-exchange entitlements to repayment, such as the sterling balances, amassed as the result of the deficits that the belligerents of the second world war incurred for imports and military expenditure while their exports were curtailed. These would have been invaluable to a country embarking on a programme of investment but they were mainly dissipated as soon as they were released in paying for excess imports of consumer goods.[5] By the time that reserves were exhausted, patterns of trade had been set up which would be politically difficult to change, and it seemed quite natural to fall back on aid to keep them open.

For the governments of so-called developing countries, to incur debt was the line of least resistance. It enabled them to talk a great deal about national growth and, indeed, to have much investment carried out, without having to mobilise a surplus within the home economy by imposing restraints upon inessential consumption. Moreover this helped them to demonstrate to Western donors that they were not infected with left-wing ideas.

Even if aid had been used in the strictest possible manner to develop the national economy, it would not necessarily have fructified in production of exportable goods to make repayment possible, especially since there were obstacles in the way of entering the markets of the donor countries; but in any case, much indebtedness was incurred for imports that impeded rather than fostered economic growth.

As debt piled up, more and more of current receipts of foreign exchange had to be used to service it. Thus a given annual amount of aid offered by donors made an ever-dwindling flow of funds to the recipients, until the situation was reached in which a great part of aid was required merely to pay for the service of aid already received. This was the paradoxical consequence of the attempt to 'transfer resources' from one country to another within

---

[5] Cf. Cheryl Payer, *The Debt Trap*, Pelican, 1974.

the framework of international commercial relationships.[6]

Governments and economists in the Third World did not take indebtedness very seriously. Many of the newly independent states seem to have felt that their ex-imperialist exploiters owed them some kind of reparations so that aid was only their due. They believed that in the end this would be recognised and the debts would never have to be repaid. Once the promised growth had been realised and the country reached the goal of economic independence, the debts would be written off, either by consent or by repudiation.

In the era described above, when an outflow of finance (mainly from Britain) was developing North America, the rules of profit-seeking private enterprise prevailed. Lenders had to judge the prospects of the borrowers' success so as to ensure that they would get their money back. If the business of a borrower was not successful, its bonds became worthless. The loss fell upon rentiers who were holding them, while any physical means of production that had been created remained on the spot and might be useful later.

Indebtedness to a foreign government or international institution does not cancel itself. Repudiation is a political act. It was often contemplated, no doubt, but always for the future because debt could not be repudiated as long as it was necessary to go on borrowing. During the 1960s (which was proclaimed to be the second Decade of Development), one country after another ran into a situation of incipient bankruptcy, that is, where its current reserves fell short of the accumulated deficit in its balance of payments; it then had to accept a composition with its creditors, postponing obligations for payment of old debt and

[6] The relation between new loans and debt service in 1967 and in 1974 were as follows:

	Loans and aid gross	Debt service	Net inflow
	billion dollars		
1967	9.7	3.9	5.8
1974	14.9	10.6	4.3

Thus, over this period, the ratio of the net receipts to gross payments fell from nearly 60 per cent to less than one third.

The overall ratio of official debt service requirements to export earnings rose over this period from 7.1 to 9.6. For many individual countries, this ratio in 1971 was between 20 and 30 per cent.

Source: UNCTAD Handbook of International Trade and Development Statistics, United Nations, 1976.

permitting new loans, on terms which involved concessions to the financial and political views of the lenders. Thus it became clear that the underlying reason for giving aid in the form of loans was not because the donors needed their money back but because it enabled them to maintain the authority of the rules of the free market system. (When OPEC suddenly turned the rules against them, they were indignant but decided that it was better to comply than to repudiate the system.)

An exception which proves the rule was provided by Ghana in 1972. A military government took power, abrogated the onerous terms of a settlement made with its predecessors and decreed its own terms for renouncing and rescheduling debts. Ghana was promptly cut off from trade credit from its usual suppliers. Imports were strictly rationed and a campaign begun to grow more food at home. To avoid a confrontation which would have put ideas into the hands of other debtors, the World Bank quickly organised a settlement on terms far more favourable to Ghana than the preceding one. Credit was restored, imports came in again, and the patriotic dash for self-reliance petered out. Ghana gained a good deal compared to meeker bankrupts, but the breach in the system of financial discipline was quickly staunched.

Role of the International Monetary Fund

In its original conception, the IMF was intended to provide international liquidity. Drawing rights allocated to a country represented an addition to its holdings of gold and other monetary reserves. The underlying conception was that when a country ran into a deficit in its balance of payments, drawing upon the Fund would bridge the gap for a time, while the monetary authorities took appropriate steps to get back into balance. In practice, the Fund's operations were completely swamped by the outflow of finance from the USA but it found a niche in the world monetary system as the supervisor over borrowing by the Third World. A continuous flow of finance to a so-called developing country is, of course, a completely different matter from a temporary drawing upon monetary reserves, but the system developed, without any consistent plan, through the interaction of the actual situation with the rules that had been laid down when the IMF was set up.

Each country is given a quota, defining its rights to draw on the Fund, which is divided into tranches (slices). The first is subscribed in gold and is at the country's disposal. The second tranche can be drawn upon subject to the consent of the managers of the Fund; to draw upon the third tranche or beyond, it has to submit to consultation with the Fund which in practice means that it must accept policies imposed upon it as a condition for renewed borrowing. The amounts that can be drawn directly from the Fund are not large but its agreement provides a kind of certificate to other lenders, while a refusal would dry up credit from the West completely.

The conditions laid down by the Fund were based on the belief that strict adherence to financial orthodoxy, a restrictive monetary policy and reliance on the operation of the free market system of prices could always be relied upon to bring about equilibrium in the balance of payments and lead to stable growth.[7]

To find the origin of these conceptions, we must consider how the gold standard system was interpreted in orthodox theory.

As we have seen, in the situation that came to an end in 1914, there was harmony, in broad terms, between flows of international finance and the pattern of deficits and surpluses in trade. For this reason, there was little strain on the international monetary system (apart from occasional crises) and fixed exchange rates for the leading countries were preserved by observing the rules of the gold standard system.

There seems no great need to depend upon a monetarist analysis to explain the relative success of the international gold standard system between the years 1896 and 1914. This was a period without major wars, and one during which the volume of international reserves (newly mined gold) was increasing at a fast rate. Furthermore, the system fostered large-scale equilibrating short-term capital transfers. As long as most economies were stable in character, and the initial exchange rates of the major trading nations were not far out of line with each other, there is no need for a *deus ex machina* to explain why the system should have functioned successfully for some twenty years. After all, a fixed exchange-rate system functioned well enough between 1949 and 1967 under conditions far less conducive to the

[7] Cf. Eprine Eshag and Rosemary Thorp, 'Economic and Social Consequences of Orthodox Economic Policies in Argentina in the Post-War Years', *Bulletin of the Oxford University Institute of Economics and Statistics,* February 1965.

successful maintenance of stability, and began to show serious signs of stress only when the internal mechanism of the system prevented the continued fast growth of acceptable international reserves.[8]

However, the gold standard and even the metal itself, got the credit for preserving equilibrium. Ricardo had laid the foundation of orthodox doctrine which was still being taught in the 1920s. He held that overseas investment was both undesirable and unlikely to occur. The foreign income account of each country consisted simply of the value of its exports and imports. When payment for imports exceeded earnings from exports, the difference was made up by drawing upon the country's stock of gold. Next, the quantity theory of money was brought into the argument. The loss of gold from the deficit country would cause prices there to fall while the gain of gold outside would raise prices abroad. Then competition between home and foreign goods would increase exports and check imports until balance was reached and the movement of gold came to an end.

The version of this doctrine that continued to prevail after the 1914–18 war was only slightly more sophisticated. In each country, a central bank or its equivalent was charged with the duty of maintaining the convertibility of its national currency with gold and therefore of preserving adequate reserves. A persistent loss of gold had to be stopped by raising the interest rate at home. This attracted lending from abroad, which set up a demand for home currency and so stopped the outflow of gold. At this stage, the country was borrowing to pay for its excess of imports. This was only a temporary relief; meanwhile the restriction of credit necessary to get the rate of interest up was reducing effective demand at home (that is, causing a slump and unemployment) and so bringing about the fall in prices necessary to eliminate the deficit in the balance of payments. (It was faith in this mechanism, which Keynes called 'hateful and disastrous', that led to the unfortunate British experiment with a restored gold standard from 1925 to 1931.[9])

In reality, the gold standard system did not operate on international balances of trade but on the differences between balances

---

[8] C. A. E. Goodhart, *The Business of Banking 1891–1941*, Weidenfeld and Nicholson, 1972, p. 220.

[9] See *The Economic Consequences of Mr. Winston Churchill*, 1925, reprinted in *Essays in Persuasion*, J. M. Keynes, *Writings*, Vol. IX.

and flows of lending. It could flourish in a period when these differences in any case were not very great. When London was the main source of overseas finance, and the British balance of foreign income was continuously in surplus (largely because of receipts of interest on former loans) the interest-rate mechanism only had to restrict or stimulate the flow of net lending to keep it approximately equal to the surplus.

A country with a persistent deficit could attract finance so long as prospective profits were sufficiently high to establish confidence in the ability of its businesses to service loans over the future. When confidence was impaired, for instance in a slump, new borrowing was sharply reduced, investment fell off and there was unemployment and falling prices. This was the discipline of the market which the IMF wants to re-establish.

The traditional bankers' view is that excessive indebtedness is the result of mismanagement for which the country should be made to suffer :

The corollary of the traditional view is the 'short leash' approach that would ensure that a debt-relief operation is a deterring and traumatic experience for the debtor – with relief extended as seldom as possible, as late as possible, and on terms that are as harsh as possible. Once again in the present context, such a response is so much at variance with the goals of development and economic stability that it contradicts the aims which the creditor countries themselves are committed to in their capacity of donors.[10]

The gold standard proved to be a fair-weather vessel. When it was re-launched in the choppy waters of the inter-war period it could not keep afloat, but belief in its supposed virtues are still used to justify 'disastrous' policies.

There are three main elements in the package of policies which the IMF imposes on a country which is seeking its aid :

First, the requirement of measures to reduce expenditure through restriction of credit, raising interest rates, reduction of budget deficits and so forth, calculated to increase unemployment, and perhaps to reduce prices.

Second, objections to any attempt to defend the interests of workers and peasants against the rigours of this policy by price controls, subsidies or support to wage rates.

Third, objections to measures intended to improve the country's

[10] UNCTAD IV TD/183, para. 106.

balance of payments by protective tariffs, systems of import licensing, multiple exchange rates favouring exports and so forth. In place of such devices, the IMF usually insists upon a devaluation of the country's currency. Where the main exports are raw materials in inelastic demand, this fails to increase foreign earnings and it pours oil on the fire of inflation at home.[11]

Is all this purely the result of dogmatism or is there some purpose behind it? The Pearson Report which reviewed the relationship between industrialised capitalist nations and the Third World in 1969, under the optimistic title *Partners in Development*, stated: 'A keynote of aid policy should be the achievement of long-term and self sustaining development.'[12] But, as it has worked out, aid policy does not seem to foster whatever efforts at self-reliance the Third World has attempted to make.

New rules

For some twenty years after the end of the second world war, the main Western nations maintained a system of fixed exchange rates between their currencies, as under the gold standard.

The US dollar ousted gold and all other currencies as an internationally acceptable means of payment. An outflow of finance from the United States (much in excess of the surplus on income account) provided sufficient supplies of liquidity for international business and enabled the Central Banks of the world to build up reserves. Europeans complained of American corporations buying up their industries and making investments to supply their markets by means of inflows of dollars that were absorbed into financial reserves and carried no counterpart in real goods and services, but so far as the monetary mechanism was concerned, the system worked smoothly.

In the latter years of the 1960s, two changes set in. First, great disparities in the balances of various countries on income account put insupportable strains upon the fixity of exchange rates. European deficit countries had to be allowed to devalue their currencies and surplus countries were obliged to appreciate.[13]

---

[11] Cf. above p. 68.
[12] *Op. cit.*, p. 124.
[13] Cf. above p. 79.

Finally, the dollar itself was devalued in an attempt to protect American industry against competition of imports, mainly from West Germany and Japan.

After various intermediate steps had been tried and failed, the IMF was obliged, in 1976, to accept the position that each country is free to set its exchange rate at whatever level it is willing and able to establish, and to allow it to float up or down without any obligation to maintain some particular value. Now all are 'floating' or rather bobbing about relatively to each other, and the dollar has ceased to be a stable unit of account.

This system is awkward for Third World countries, which have receipts and obligations expressed in various national currencies, and they would much prefer the establishment of a single world currency.

During the 1960s there were discussions of the possibility of creating a genuinely international currency to provide for Central Bank reserves. This consisted of 'special drawing rights' in the IMF which would supply the monetary authorities of the world with, so to speak, synthetic gold which they could use to make payments to each other. Quotas of SDRs, expressed in gold dollars, were first issued in 1969. Drawing rights are now expressed in terms of an index of the value of the 16 most important currencies, so that their variations relative to each other cancel out. A system based on SDRs would suit the needs of the Third World better than any other that has yet been evolved. First of all, it would provide a base in which their own exchange rates with all Western currencies could be established and the value of their own reserves stabilised. Secondly, the allocation of SDRs would be on a system of quotas which would provide a more rational distribution of reserves than that which comes about through the distribution of gold thrown up by the accidents of history. Finally, there was a proposal for a 'link' between SDRs and aid to the Third World so that whenever the rich countries needed an increase in the total of international liquidity, provided by an all round increase of SDRs, there would be an automatic provision of interest-free loans to Third World authorities.

To set afloat a new form of money requires the establishment of confidence in it. Unfortunately the countries that have large stocks of actual gold have not shown much eagerness to support the system of SDRs as synthetic gold to take its place. The amount of SDRs so far created is very small in relation to the requirements of international liquidity and it appears that the old yellow metal is still a formidable rival to any rational scheme that can be provided. But in 1978, the depreciation of the US dollar was making the need for reform more painfully obvious than ever.

Debts and credits

A second change that began to set in in the late 1960s was a fall off in American foreign lending (though the outflow of dollars for the expenses of the Vietnam war was increasing). There was, however, a great increase in private commercial lending, a part of which came to Third World countries through transnational corporations or by direct public and private sector borrowing.

Commercial credit was largely provided through the Euro-dollar market. This financial market is constituted by the operations of banks with international connections, domiciled in Europe, which accept deposits and make loans in terms of American dollars and other national currencies. Just as in the banking system of a single country, loans create deposits and deposits are available to lend. So long as banks could find what appeared to be credit-worthy borrowers the creation of international purchasing power could go on without limit, unchecked by reserve ratio requirements or the discipline of a Central Bank.

The United States was running its overseas war without checking home activity, on the principle that their economy was able to provide guns *and* butter.

This contributed to a world-wide inflationary boom, in which the Third World shared to a certain extent. Some countries were being paid for contributing to the American war effort, some offering hospitality to transnational investment, some raising commercial loans for themselves and nearly all benefiting from the high demand for primary commodities.

The slump of 1974 brought the usual reaction on their terms of trade and the raised price of oil made a large addition to their bills for imports. All Third World countries outside OPEC were plunged into still greater deficits and were obliged to borrow at a faster rate than they had been able to do during the boom.

In 1976, the total outstanding debt of the 'less developed countries' was reckoned to be $130 billion, of which about $25 billion was held by commercial banks.[14] In March 1978 it was estimated at $250 billion and was continuing to grow.

The overall current account deficit of what became known as the 'non-oil developing countries' rose from $11 billion in 1973 to $38 billion in 1975, and has been running between $25 and $30 billion per annum since then.[15]

Debt service is a severe burden on balances of payments. Restrictive monetary policies have to be imposed and plans for growth cut back in order to keep down the level of imports.

This situation is by no means helpful to the functioning of the capitalist market. First, the restriction of purchases from the Third World is limiting the market for exports, which is disadvantageous particularly to those Western countries which are themselves suffering from trade deficits. Secondly, the possibility of defaults is a threat to the solvency of highly respected banks that have lent too rashly and so to the whole structure of the Western financial system.

In discussions between the rich and poor countries over the problem of debt, the representatives of the creditors are in one dilemma – how to make demands for payment manageable without letting the borrowers off too lightly, and the debtors are in another – how to get out of their obligations without drying up the sources of credit for the future.

The financial authorities of the Western world have learned a great deal from former crises; they may be expected to find a way through this one, though not necessarily a way that is propitious to development in the Third World.

Meanwhile, the deficit on income account of the United States was being more than covered by an inflow of lending from those members of OPEC who could find no better use for their export earnings. Should this not be counted as 'aid' to America, from the Arab States?

[14] World Bank News Service, 1 March, 1976.
[15] *IMF Survey,* 5 January, 1976 and 19 September, 1977.

6

DEPENDENT INDUSTRIALISATION

The most pervasive and strongly held of all neoclassical doctrines is that of the universal benefits of free trade, but unfortunately the theory in terms of which it is expounded has no relevance to the question that it purports to discuss. The argument is conducted in terms of comparisons of static equilibrium positions in which each trading nation is enjoying full employment of all resources and balanced payments, the flow of exports, valued at world prices, being equal to the flow of imports. In such conditions, there is no motive for resorting to protection of home industry. Since full employment of given resources is assumed, there is no need for protection to increase home industry, and since timeless equilibrium is assumed there can never be a deficit in the balance of payments. Moreover, since all countries are treated as having the same level of development, there can be no question of 'unequal exchange'.

Free trade theory

Modern teaching is still based upon the case that Ricardo made against protective tariffs in England in the early nineteenth century. The classical argument against protection was that it produces a misallocation of resources inside the country that imposes it. Ricardo's analysis of *comparative advantage* is often misunderstood. The comparison is not between the costs of production, in money terms, of particular commodities at home and abroad; it is a comparison between the real costs (in terms of labour time and other resources) of different commodities at home. The argument was that, when protection is taken off, resources will move from the production of commodities with high real costs (which can then be imported) to those with lower real costs, so that the total productivity is increased. This argument applies when all resources are always employed. It has no force for a country with massive unemployment where the potential surplus is far from being fully realised. Moreover, the argument requires the assumption that exports pay for imports so that an increase in the value of imports (following the removal of protection) will automatically be accompanied by a corresponding increase in exports of the commodities in which the country concerned has a comparative advantage. In fact, the value of exports for any one Third World country largely depends on the state of demand in the world market for whatever primary commodities it can sell (and on the prices offered by rival suppliers).

The argument for free trade based on 'comparative real costs' also implies that a movement of resources from one line of production to another can take place smoothly, without losses or conflicts of interest within the country where the movement takes place. The developed industrial countries themselves find this assumption quite inappropriate; they frequently make use of protection to save particular groups of businesses and workers from having to move out of an established line of production when it is threatened by competition from cheap imports.

The most misleading feature of the classical case for free trade (and the arguments based upon it in modern textbooks) is that it is purely static. It is set out in terms of a comparison of the productivity of *given* resources (fully employed) with or without trade. Ricardo took the example of trade between England and Portugal. He argued that England, by allowing imports of wine from Portugal, would expand the production and export of cloth to pay for it. Ricardo, of course, was thinking of the English side of the exchange but the analysis is perfectly symmetrical; it implies that Portugal will gain from specialising on wine and importing cloth. In reality, the imposition of free trade on Portugal killed off a promising textile industry and left her with a slow-growing export market for wine, while for England, exports of cotton cloth led to accumulation, mechanisation and the whole spiralling growth of the industrial revolution.[1]

[1] Cf. S. Sideri, *Trade and Power: Informal Colonialism in Anglo-Portuguese Relations,* Rotterdam, 1970.

Free trade for *other* countries is obviously an advantage for an exporting nation. Ricardo's doctrine was very convenient for England at that time, but soon Germany, the United States and Japan began to develop industries (at first behind tariff walls) which demonstrated that static comparative advantage is a very poor guide to the possibilities of industrial development.

The free-trade doctrine was part of the general defence of laisser faire. Protection is an interference with the free play of market forces. For this reason, the doctrine suits the interests of whichever nation is in the strongest competitive position in world markets. Under the British Empire, the imposition of free trade made it possible for the Lancashire cotton industry first to ruin hand-loom production in what is now the Third World, and later to hamper the growth of capitalism on the spot. In the post-war period, American influence was exercised, directly and through various international agencies, in favour of free trade but since Japan became the strongest industrial competitor, faith in the doctrine has begun to weaken in the United States.

Protective practice

The economists of the Third World who have been brought up in the Western tradition absorbed the doctrine of the universal benefits of free trade and did not realise its irrelevance to their situation but governments embarking upon development everywhere have adopted policies of high protection. This was partly because, after their war-time balances had been exhausted, and the Korean war boom had collapsed, they experienced an acute shortage of foreign exchange[2] and partly because they regarded industrialisation as the clue to prosperity and wanted to encourage home production of substitutes for imports.

Industrialisation in several Latin American countries began as a process of import substitution when their export earnings collapsed in the slump of the 1930s. (Even the British allowed India to impose import duties on cotton textiles at that time.) The same policy was revived and spread to newly independent countries in Asia after the second world war.

Economists in the West scold the Third World for adopting

[2] Cf. above, p. 92.

protection.[3] Their objections are based, first of all, on Ricardo's argument that protection draws resources into activities with higher real costs compared to others. For developing countries, the problem is to use their resources of manpower for something or other, since they have a massive reserve of unemployment, and need to build up resources by investment. For them, the static comparative advantage argument is quite beside the point.

The free-traders believe that it would have been possible for the countries concerned to make sufficient exports of manufactures to balance their trade without protection. This belief is based upon dogma rather than on an examination of the state of world markets.

They argue that a lower exchange rate is a better method than protection of balancing trade, for it offers a premium to exporters in terms of home currency.[4] They fail to observe that traditional exports of primary products generally suffer from inelastic total demand, so that a lower exchange rate only gives one seller a competitive advantage over others, and all together lose foreign earnings.[5]

Finally, they observe that agriculture has been neglected so that exports of cash crops have been kept down.

Underlying the arguments of the free traders is still the same (perhaps unconscious) bias towards the interests of their homeland in the West that made Ricardo recommend Portugal to give up its textile industry and specialise on wine.

It is certainly true that agriculture in the Third World has been too much neglected, but this it not because industry has been too much favoured but because the social and political changes necessary to modernise agriculture have not been made.

There are many detailed criticisms of the type of industrial development fostered by protection. Initially, import saving is attempted by installing only the final assembly stage of production, say of motor cars, while all the ingredients have to be imported. The cost in terms of foreign exchange has then often been found to be greater than the cost of importing the car ready made. However, in a country such as India, that has some basic

[3] See I. Little, T. Scitovsky and M. Scott, *Industry & Trade in Some Developing Countries,* Oxford University Press, 1970.
[4] Cf. below, p. 107.
[5] Cf. above, p. 68.

industry of its own, the import-saving process can gradually work back until the almost whole car is home-made.

The free traders observe that a genuinely home-made car, produced under high protection, costs the citizen of the country several times the world price, but this is beside the point for to buy at the world price would add to the deficit in the country's balance of trade which import-saving investment is intended to relieve.

Industries set up under protection have often been found to run at a very low level of capacity. Multiple shifts are rarely used and daily output is often at less than half designed capacity of a single shift.[6] This means the cost of the investment has been extravagant relatively both to output and to employment offered. Low utilisation is partly to be accounted for by lack of demand and partly by the difficulty of importing the materials required to operate the plant and spare parts to maintain it; in some cases, also, by the host country allowing many competitors to set up plants, so that none can enjoy the economies of scale appropriate to the whole market.

Furthermore, the methods of protection that were adopted were not such as to promote self-reliant development and an attack on poverty and unemployment. Frequently these controls result in a distribution of income and an allocation of investment that is even worse than the free trade situation.

Pakistan is a good example, though many other countries can be shown to have followed similar policies. Planners argued that free trade was no good. They set up a system of multiple exchange rates, direct licensing of imports and arbitrary subsidies on exports (through an export bonus scheme). Some of the results were as follows:

On the argument that the demand for raw jute was inelastic the growers of raw jute, the major export, were offered the most unfavourable rate of exchange. A dollar earned by the jute growers, usually small farmers, received Rs 5.

At the same time, it was argued that the demand for jute goods was elastic and the jute manufacturers, big capitalists, were offered a very favourable rate of exchange, Rs 10 per dollar earned.

---

[6] *Ibid,* p. 93 et seq.

The traders, often the capitalists themselves, received import licences for which foreign exchange was made available at the artificially low official rate (Rs 5 to the dollar). Since these imports were strictly licensed there was a huge scarcity premium on them which was appropriated by the traders. Thus the peasants probably paid Rs 15 for the imported consumer goods purchased against dollars for which they received only Rs 5. The system was designed to redistribute income in favour of the capitalists and traders.[7]

Free-traders like Little, Scitovsky and Scott dismiss the above cases as mistakes by the planners. They fail to see that these policies are instruments to achieve the objectives of the planners, such as redistribution of proceeds from trade in favour of the rich.

Even when the import-saving investments have been successful and plant is operated at capacity, the technique for which plant is designed has an unnecessarily high capital to labour ratio, and in some cases has taken the market away from local small-scale labour-intensive industries, thus actually reducing employment. By the same token, the high share of profits and big salaries in these industries tends to exacerbate inequality. All these imperfections flow, not from industrialisation as such, but, first, from the planners' choice of investment projects on the basis of 'willingness to pay', say, for passenger cars, and secondly from imitating Western industry and allowing or inviting Western businesses to organise industry for them.

Far eastern miracles

In contrast to unsatisfactory protective policies, the free-traders are fond of pointing to the success of certain small countries, particularly Hong Kong, Taiwan and South Korea, in building up export business. Low wages do not necessarily mean cheap labour, but it seems that in these countries workers are exceptionally patient, dextrous and well disciplined, so that low wages give their employers a powerful competitive advantage in export markets. Since they are in competition with each other in keeping

[7] See Keith Griffin and Azizur Rahman Khan, *Growth and Inequality in Pakistan,* Macmillan, 1972.

down costs, the authorities try to avoid the expenses involved in social services.

An American reporter observes that in Hong Kong administrators fear that social programmes might have the effect of driving away potential investors.

These services are very expensive, says a government appointed urban councillor sombrely. If Hong Kong wants to provide them, taxes will go up and investment will go down. More medical services, for example, would reduce the competitiveness of Hong Kong industry.

The results have produced a social system thin enough to be skeletal. Hong Kong has no form of unemployment compensation, and most companies pay their staffs only when there is a day's work to perform. The hardest hit are construction and other outdoor workers, who daily travel to their job sites but work only if weather permits. When it does not, they go home unpaid. There is no minimum wage law, and child-labour restrictions apply only to anyone under the age of 14. Free schooling is provided only up to the age of eleven.

Medical benefits are equally non-existent, although infirmity loans are available for anyone over the age of 70. Otherwise the 4.3 million population is served by only five public hospitals, one for psychiatric cases. Nearly half the population lives in public-housing flats, 80 per cent of which have no water, private toilets or kitchen facilities. Yet 450,000 new apartments are still needed. Private housing is almost as woeful. 140,000 families are registered as living in overcrowded conditions, 40,000 in inadequate buildings and 170,000 in squatter huts.[8]

The case of Taiwan is somewhat less discouraging because of its historical background. The peasants of Taiwan had been well drilled in modern methods of cultivation under the former Japanese administration.

It was tacitly assumed, and even frequently expressed by experts at the Taipei agricultural station research bureau that police power had to be employed to force new farming techniques on to rural communities resisting change. One observer evaluated the police force's role in these terms: In each district throughout the island the chief of police exercised the power to protect and change traditional behaviour as well as introduce new customs and ideas, he also was dedicated to stimulating industry and increasing the wealth of his area and laying the groundwork for a new communication system. There are many benefits to be derived in this way for developing an area. Since the police penetrated to every village household through the ho-ko (pao-chia) system it was relatively easy for them to insist on the adoption of new sugar cane or rice seeds and supervise their use.[9]

[8] *Time*, 20 December, 1976.

[9] Ramon H. Myers and Adrienne Ching, 'Agricultural development in Taiwan under Japanese colonial rule', *Journal of Asian Studies*, Vol. xxiii, No. 4, August 1964. The quotation is from a publication in Taiwan of 1919.

The Kuomintang forces had fought a long war in the side of landlords on the mainland of China, but on the island of Taiwan they made a thorough-going land reform. They had been met by a revolt of the inhabitants when they arrived, and after suppressing it, they found the best way to stablise their position was to throw out the local landlords and distribute small but viable holdings to the peasants. Thereafter, marketing and production were regulated by setting the price of fertiliser in terms of rice.

Within industry, emphasis was placed initially on small and medium sized firms which used labour-intensive techniques of production. The rapid expansion of these industries was associated with rapid growth of employment opportunities in urban areas. In consequence, real wages rose quickly in both sectors . . . income inequality was reduced and the urban–rural wage differential practically vanished—the only country in Asia, and perhaps in the whole of the Third World, where this has occurred.[10]

As in Japan, an alien military dictatorship was more effective in creating the preconditions for prosperous peasant agriculture than any native Third World government has been. (The free-traders praise Taiwan for subsequently developing export industries, but she has been able to maintain a continuous large import surplus offset by gifts and loans on favourable terms, in early years, up to 40 per cent of her total import bill.)[11]

In South Korea, wages are even lower and discipline harsher than in the other two. Heavy and light industry have been built up, largely financed by American and Japanese corporations to fabricate imported materials. For instance, the South Korean steel industry is fed by American scrap. Formerly, South Korea was the 'rice bowl' of the peninsula, but now it is heavily dependent on imported food. In spite of formidable competitive power in exports, South Korea has never succeeded in achieving balanced trade; the economy is maintained by loans and subventions and the government has to rely on its 'strategic value' for continued support from the USA.

If development means overcoming poverty and building up

Quoted by K. N. Raj in 'Some Questions Concerning Growth, Transformation and Planning of Agriculture in Developing Countries', *Journal of Development Planning*, No. 1, United Nations, 1969.

[10] Keith Griffin, 'Policy Options in Rural Development', *Oxford University Bulletin of Economics and Statistics*, Vol. 35, 1973.

[11] Little et al., *op. cit.*, p. 53.

national self-reliance, these miracles can hardly be regarded as examples of success.

Transnational finance

The greater part of capitalist investment in what is now the Third World first came from overseas.

There was some investment in manufactures, financed from the metropolis, in the European empires; and, as we have seen, in Latin America in the 1930s, loss of export earnings led to high protection which induced some foreign firms, from which imports had been coming before the slump, to jump over the tariff wall and set up at least the final stages of production in the country where their market lay. Since decolonisation, and particularly since the end of the 1950s, this type of investment has been growing rapidly, mainly in the form of setting up branch plants by the transnational corporations, sometimes in conjunction with local capitalists, in the peripheral countries.

The pressure towards overseas investment came from within the industrial economies; most of it was directed to growing specialisation and the interpenetration of each other's industry but there was also an overspill to some parts of the Third World where markets appeared promising.

The mechanism of capitalism is that a successful business has profits to invest in expanding its operations, and when its credit is established it can borrow as well. The limit on its expansion does not come from lack of finance but from the market in its homeland for the range of commodities that it produces. Therefore it is continually searching for new things to produce. An outlet for earlier generations of commodities is then advantageous. The research and development has all been done, the technology and designs tried out and often the actual equipment can be moved and given a new lease of life in supplying a fresh market with a labour force recruited and trained to work it.

Since the end of the 1950s, when the flow of aid fell off with disillusionment and fatigue amongst the main donors,[12] they attempted to salve their conscience with the argument that direct investment had taken over the task of development from them.

[12] UNCTAD IV T/D 188.

However, the finance coming into Third World countries from the transnational corporations cannot be regarded as a transfer of resources to the poor countries from the rich. The reverse is the case. In the early 1970s remittance of profits from old investment and payments required to service old loans (apart from OPEC) much exceeded new investments. Taking the Third World as a whole, the great corporations are extracting surplus from them rather than transferring 'capital' to them.

During 1970–73 the ratio of *net* investment income payments abroad by the developing countries as a group to *net* direct foreign investment including re-invested earnings of foreign firms and other long-term private capital flows was 3.6.[13]

In other words, during the period 1970–73 *outflows* of resources from the developing countries through remittances of profits, dividends, management fees and royalties, etc., were 3.6 times larger than the inflows of resources through foreign private investment and other long-term private capital flows.

After 1973 the outflow from OPEC distorts the picture as this part of the Third World is now a creditor, not a debtor, to the West.

In 1972, payments, excluding the OPEC countries, were 2.3 times the new direct investment, including that financed out of profits made in the Third World countries, and in 1974, 1.6 times.

It is to be observed that investment out of retained earnings brings no new finance to the country concerned but the capital so created ranks for remission of profits along with that which results from an inflow of funds.

Transplanting industry

The greater part of what purported to be import-saving investment was carried out by transnational corporations, sometimes by direct investment under their own management, sometimes in conjunction with local business, and sometimes under management fees and licensing under patents.

The process generally began by former exporters offering to

[13] UNCTAD, *Handbook of International Trade and Development Statistics,* Geneva, 1976, Table 5.1, p. 272.

carry out the last stage of assembly in the host country and continuing to export the ingredients. This accounts for the fact that such 'import saving' often increases the country's foreign exchange bill. In an industrially weak economy, such as that of Kenya, this still goes on, but in a country which already has some basis for investment industry, intermediate products also begin to be produced there and some genuine saving of imports occurs.

The choice of what imports to save is partly influenced by the local government and business interests and partly by the convenience of the transnational investors. Profit-seeking enterprise must start from an existing market. The process of import substitution naturally begins with the commodities that offer the best prospects of profit, that is, those which are bought by the wealthest consumers. Thus import substitution has fostered the production of motor cars and other consumer durables.

The nature of the objects to be produced determines, within a narrow range, the technique of production and the type of investment required to produce them. The high capital to labour ratio in such plants is accounted for by the fact that they embody highly mechanised techniques of production, pioneered in the West in conditions of scarcity of labour, and the low level of utilisation is due to the large minimum size of investment required to produce such outputs at all. In physical terms, the output to capital ratio is lower in the branch plant than at home but the cost of capital to the transnational corporation is lower because the research and development were paid for long ago, and sometimes the physical equipment is secondhand.

The level of wages in these plants is usually somewhat higher than the local level. This enables the branch managers to pick out the most experienced and the most docile workers and helps to ensure their loyalty to their employers. However, because of the high level of mechanisation, the share of wages in value added is lower than in local industry in general and the share of profits and high salaries greater. This kind of investment therefore increases the inequality of income where it operates, and so helps to generate demand for its own products. The famous 'miracle' of Brazil, which is discussed below, was an example of this pattern of industrialisation.

Transnational investment is not confined to import substitution but also caters for the home market wherever it can find profitable openings. Such investment often begins by buying up a business that already exists. For instance, in Mexico, from 1956 to 1967, only one third of transnational investment was in setting up new factories.[14] The plant, the labour force and a place in the market are taken over. This leads to a more intense competition with local business in the same line. New methods of management and labour discipline may or may not be more efficient in lowering costs, but there is one respect in which the new branch business will far and away excel the one that it displaces – that is, in salesmanship. Customers will quickly be convinced that what they are now buying is very much superior to what was available before.[15] Once the corporation has captured the market, there will be no chance for local producers to come back into it.

Consumers' preferences

The respect for 'consumers' sovereignty' has always been a weak point in orthodox economic theory even at home; in the Third World it has been made ridiculous by the snob value attached to foreign goods and by the power of advertisement, which can induce consumers to substitute modern products even for mothers' milk.

The Nestlé libel case highlighted this point.

In response to a pamphlet entitled 'Nestlé Kills Babies', published in 1974 by the Swiss consumer/activist group, *Arbeitsgruppe Dritte Welt*, Nestle Alimentana filed a four-count libel suit against members of the organization. The pamphlet was a reprint of an earlier one entitled 'Bottled Babies' published by a similar British group. Both alleged that false advertising had prompted mothers in LDCs to use infant formula instead of breast feeding, and consequently caused the deaths of thousands of children. However the original pamphlet had not mentioned Nestlé or any of the other companies by name, and thus did not raise the issue of libel.

Three of the charges, which Nestlé subsequently withdrew, related to allegations made in the pamphlet about Nestlé's promotional methods in LDCs. The fourth charge which led to a judgment against thirteen members of the group in June 1976, focused on the defamatory title—'Nestlé Kills Babies'.

[14] See 'The impact of multinational enterprise on employment and training', ILO, 1976, p. 9.
[15] Cf. R. I. Barnet and R. E. Muller, *Global Reach*, Simon and Schuster, New York, 1974, p. 172 et seq.

In his decision, the judge stated that the cause behind the injuries and deaths was not Nestlé's products; rather, it was the unhygienic way they were prepared by end-users. Although Nestlé won its case, the firm's victory was diluted by (1) having to pay one third of the court costs and (2) being told by the judge to change its marketing methods to prevent further misuse of its products. The defendants were ordered to pay $120 each in damages to Nestlé and two thirds of court costs.[16]

The judge's advice could not have been of much use to the mothers who were the end-users of the milk powder since their unhygienic way of preparing it was due to the absence of clean water where they lived. In any case, the main charge against Nestle was making propaganda against breast-feeding in order to generate a market for its own products.

During the great boom in consumer durables in Brazil, representatives of the transnational investors were at first worried by the effect that the display of ever-new luxuries would have upon the minds of the growing mass of families with no means to buy even the barest necessities, but recent investigations have reassured them. It seems that advertising mesmerises even the shanty dwellers into believing that they are sharing in the growth of prosperity. (A salesman for furniture polish visiting hovels with mud floors was often told, 'I don't have a floor to wax, but I can buy the wax if I want to.')[17]

The intrusion of Western production into a pre-capitalist economy begins by ruining the local producers (as Lancashire piece-goods ruined the handloom weavers of India) and, where there is little scope for expanding the market, the new investment makes no appreciable increase in total productive capacity. The salt industry in Ghana provides an example. In the nineteenth century, production and marketing of salt was a profitable activity employing thousands of Ghanaians directly, and requiring ancillary activities such as building canoes. The introduction of a modern mechanised salt works took away the whole market and destroyed the livelihood of all who depended on the traditional industry, substituting a small amount of wage employment and, presumably, a satisfactory flow of net profit on the investment. For consumers, there is the benefit of the satisfaction of a prefer-

---

[16] *Business International,* 6 October, 1976.
[17] Barnet and Muller, *op. cit.,* p. 172 et seq.

ence for whiter salt.[18] Similarly, a mechanised bakery, in an East African city, destroys the value of the productive capacity and skill of small-scale bakers while satisfying the consumers' taste for something foreign and up-to-date.

According to the doctrine of consumers' sovereignty, since buyers prefer the Western products, there is a gain in welfare from supplying them. This gain (if any) has to be set against the loss of receipts of the old-fashioned producers and loss of national income due to unemployment.

Technology and employment

The effects of the intrusion of Western industry are felt even in countries which have reached a sophisticated level of industry of their own, for the West is continuously running ahead. Branch plants set up in Third World countries, not only introduce new commodites glamorised by salesmanship, but also new methods of production that are more mechanised than those which they displace, thus offering less employment than the average per unit of investment. To take an example once more from Mexico, in 1971 the share of transnationals in sales in the manufacturing sector of the economy was 25 per cent while the share of employment was 9.9 per cent.[19]

Indian experience provides many examples of the manner in which both aspects of foreign influence in local production are combined. In collaboration, the foreign management dominates the Indian business and succeeds in manipulating the market in such a way as to create demand for products which can be produced by their own capital-using processes.[20]

The relation of technology to employment involves a serious dilemma. (Here we are considering the demand for labour generated by a stock of capital equipment after it has been created, not the 'Keynesian' effect on employment while investment is going on.[21]) Import-saving investment, in itself, increases

[18] See T. A. Kofi, 'Abibirin Strategy of Development', *Universitas* (University of Ghana), May 1976.

[19] ILO, 1976, p. 9.

[20] Cf. K. K. Subramanian, *Import of Capital and Technology*, New Delhi, People's Publishing House, 1972, Chapter VI.

[21] See above, p. 30.

employment in the country where it takes place, while mechanising home industry, in itself, reduces employment. Should this be considered a drawback? After all, the object of investment is to create industrial capacity and raise the productivity of labour, not to 'make work' for the unemployed.

If investment were directed by a rational plan, it could be used to make the maximum feasible increase in the productivity of labour while providing the desirable level of employment. Investible resources (whether home or foreign) are extremely scarce relatively to the needs of all-round development and they should not be wasted on commodities for which capital-saving methods of production are feasible, say, in small-scale local business. The Chinese principle of walking on both legs means that investment is allocated to lines where it makes the greatest practicable net increase in productive capacity. In heavy industry and long-range transport, a high ratio of capital stock to men employed is necessary. There the increase in productivity due to mechanisation is indefinitely great, for almost nothing could be produced without it. In the general run of consumer goods and services for the mass of the population (department II) mechanisation is mainly in substitution for small-scale production. It should be postponed until all-round full employment is achieved. In these lines 'widening' is to be preferred to 'deepening' the stock of means of production, that is to say, more employment at a low level of mechanisation adds to production more than an increase in mechanisation for a small part of the labour force. Thus the slogan, walking on both legs, may be translated as maximum possible economy of investible resources to secure desired growth of ouput, and this entails the maximum possible increase in employment per unit of investment.

As it is, the choice of what lines to mechanise is left to profit-seeking corporations which, in the nature of the case, cannot work on any rational plan, and which, moreover, generally transmit abroad a large part of the additional surplus that they extract from the business. Insofar as the transnational 'transfer of capital' has merely displaced local production for the local market it cannot be regarded as a contribution to development.

The Brazilian model

Industrialisation by transplanting mechanised methods of production pioneered in the West increases employment less than would the same amount of investment conducted on the principle of walking on both legs, but it does not necessarily reduce employment absolutely – that depends upon the extent to which the process is carried on. To install productive capacity embodying advanced technology, organisation of business and training of labour, increases the flow of physical output and the value of sales (as well as squalor and smog). When it takes place sufficiently rapidly, it increases employment as well.

There are certain features of the Brazilian economy that made it particularly susceptible to this kind of development. There was a wealthy class who had become accustomed to consume imported manufactures; they were a small proportion of the population, but, in such a large country, they were sufficient to make a market for the kind of commodity that requires large-scale production; as the strongest member, Brazil had gained from participating in the Latin American Free Trade Area; the foundation for industrialisation had been laid by nationalised basic industry and the mass of the population was kept in its place by a repressive regime.

In the 1960s the transnationals came in with designs pioneered for the American market and, in alliance with national business, rapidly developed productive capacity for reproducing them. Between 1968 and 1974 there was a strong boom, growing mainly around the production of consumer durables – motor cars and electric gadgets being the main items.

The requisite import surplus was offset by the finance for direct investment by the transnational corporations as well as commercial borrowing for, while the boom lasted, credit was high.

Part of the finance was raised locally; fiscal measures reinforced the inequality of income and encouraged the acquisition of equities by the urban middle class.[22] Thus there was a growing stream of interest and profits for local rentiers; and personnel for the technostructure, recruited and trained in the country, received

[22] Celso Furtado, 'The Brazilian Model', *Social and Economic Studies* (Kingston, Jamaica), March 1973.

high salaries. These incomes helped to maintain the market for luxuries. It is a special feature of this type of development that it requires great inequality of income to begin with and that it increases inequality as it goes on. The high incomes necessary to provide purchasers for the products are themselves generated in the process of production.

The luxury products, however, were not sold only to the top 10 per cent of the income pyramid. There was also some acquisition of these goods, helped by hire-purchase credit, by households of skilled workers. Over a run of eight years, there was a huge rise in industrial employment and a sharp increase in the differential spread of wage rates.[23] There was also a great increase in employment of women (largely in service trades) so that many working-class households had several earners. At the same time, real wages for unskilled workers fell and there was an increase in 'informal' self-employment in the cities.[24] Demand for old-fashioned wage goods, such as boots and shirts, fell off and there was a disastrous fall in urban services.[25]

Towards the end of the uprush, internal strains began to appear. There was no longer any formerly under-used capacity available in basic industry and heavy investment would have been needed to keep growth going. Then, in 1974, the capitalist world slump caused a fall in export earnings for all the Third World outside OPEC, impaired credit (even for miraculous Brazil) and cast doubt upon the prospects for this particular form of industrialisation for the future.

Export platforms

A new type of transnational investment grew rapidly over the 1960s. This was directed to the employment of cheap labour, particularly in East Asia, for the output of goods to be exported to the homeland of the corporations and other industrialised countries. The countries receiving this investment have been des-

---

[23] Cf. S. A. Morley, ILO, WEP, 2–23/WP 43.

[24] Cf. above, p. 6.

[25] To take a single example, the proportion of houses in Sao Paulo with piped water fell from 71.6 per cent in 1961 to 55.7 per cent in 1971. See John Wells, 'Diffusion of Durables in Brazil', *Cambridge Journal of Economics,* September 1977.

cribed as export platforms for the corporations concerned. There are two main branches of this activity. The first is production of goods for which the advantage of mechanisation over hand-work is relatively small, such as toys, clothing and handbags; the second is breaking up complex production into stages and carrying out those that are susceptible to labour-intensive production where labour is cheap.

The attraction, for the transnational investors, of this type of production, is, first of all, the differential in wage rates. In 1970, earnings per hour for similar work in the USA were more than ten times those in Taiwan or Singapore,[26] and the cost of labour was further reduced by long hours and by the absence of any need to provide decent conditions of work.[27] Secondly, in the small East Asian countries, notably South Korea as we have seen, there is a labour force already broken-in to factory production, exceptionally dextrous and docile. And thirdly, there are strong dictatorships which do not tolerate unrest. The same type of development is taking place in Central America and the Caribbean, though there these advantages are less pronounced. Japanese corporations, as well as in East Asia, have begun to develop some subsidiaries in the Indian subcontinent and elsewhere in Asia. (On top of enjoying cheap labour, they are trying to move pollution out of their homeland.)

This kind of development is resented by workers in industrial centres from which employment is attracted away; they see it as a reaction of the corporations against the high level of wages that the labour movement in the West has succeeded in winning for them and which they regard as their due. It also sets up competition between Third World countries in keeping wage rates down. If a labour movement ever seemed liable to develop in one of these countries, the business could easily be switched to another.

The 'host' countries enjoy the advantage that employment is being organised for them but they gain only a small part of the surplus that employment produces, for the goods are shipped away valued at cost; almost the whole profit on their sale accrues abroad. For the authorities in many countries, overwhelmed by

[26] ILO, 1976, p. 13.
[27] Cf. above, p. 108.

E

unemployment, this certainly appears better than nothing, but it is obvious that this kind of business cannot lead on to self-reliant national development.

In fact, overall – extractive industry, manufactures for the local market and manufactures for sale in the centre – the Third World is actually contributing far more to the profits of the transnational corporations than it receives from them by way of new finance. Far from 'transferring capital' to the Third World, the corporations are abstracting a great part of the potential investible surplus from them, and, moreover, directing the part that they do re-invest towards their own ends – the extraction of more profit – not towards the needs of development for the countries concerned.

However, partly through collaboration with the transnational corporations, partly through investment fostered by aid and by their own public sector planning, several nations in the Third World have now built up a considerable basis in heavy industry and engineering and have laid the foundation for a continuing growth of modern production. Unfortunately for them, they now have to share in the feeble world recovery from the sharp slump of 1974, but it seems that, for instance, India and Brazil, are in a fair way to become capitalist centres of the second rank, supplying industrial products to Third World countries at an earlier stage of industrialisation.

There is no hope, even if the growth of population tapers off, of reaching full employment on this path within the foreseeable future and the very success of this type of growth builds up powerful interests among capitalists, middle-class consumers and the industrial workers as well, which put up resistance to the claims which are nowadays being expressed for a line of development based on human needs.

7

ARMAMENTS

Any help that the industrial nations have given to the countries of the Third World, in finance and technology, is far and away outweighed by the damage caused by drawing them into the Cold War and the arms race.[1]

Supply

During the period when the policy of the USA (supported, more or less, by Western Europe) was to surround the USSR with military bases, several Asian countries were taken into alliances and helped to arm themselves. Presumably, the Pentagon did not seriously rely, for instance, on the forces of Pakistan to provide a bulwark against the Red Army, but the geographical position made them convenient. (The famous U2 that was shot down in 1959 was launched from Pakistan.) Establishing a base went with providing sophisticated armaments and training the local forces to use them. The military dictatorship in Pakistan was eager to receive them, with a view to threatening India. India therefore had to arm in reply. Thus any positive aid to Pakistan was negative aid to India. India at first maintained the policy of non-alignment and paid for the arms she acquired but after stumbling into a disastrous war with China, she appealed to the West to supply her with new defence forces, which in turn were used against Pakistan.

At first the USSR supplied arms only within the socialist camp but, after the mid 1950s, she also joined the game. Soon all over Asia and North Africa, any nation could get itself armed by one or other of the great powers, and a few by both.

The motives of both great powers in arming small states lie

[1] The following argument is mainly taken from *The Arms Trade with the Third World*, SIPRI, 1971.

mainly in their manoeuvres against each other. To provide arms to a client is to acquire political influence. The advantage, for the donors, of highly sophisticated arms – especially warplanes – is that they require frequent replacement of spare parts. A client state which has been given a particular type of hardware is then dependent on the donor to maintain it. But dependence cuts both ways. A donor becomes identified with its client and cannot allow it to be defeated even when it embarks on adventures that the donor disapproves of.

For the smaller Western states, the motives for arms sales are mainly commercial. An arms industry involves very heavy investment and for the limited amount of output required at home the overheads are very high. Thus one reason for selling arms is simply to relieve pressure on the budget. Even the innocent Swedes have sometimes felt obliged to export arms for this reason, though they cut off supplies when shooting starts. Moreover, in the Mercantilist world, every nation is hungry for exports. With spare capacity, and eager buyers, it is impossible to resist the temptation to sell arms, even to potential enemies.

In an obvious sense, armaments generate war. Any nation, in a region where others are armed, would become a prey if it did not prepare for defence; from the point of view of such a nation, arms are a means to prevent war, but from the point of view of the region as a whole, they promote it.

First, any nation which has an army has an embryonic military–industrial complex. Where there is a military government, it will take all it can get hold of, both of home resources and of imports, to build up the forces on which it depends; a civilian government is often obliged to devote a large share of its budget to the military merely to placate them and persuade them not to take over so that they can help themselves.

A military establishment needs a *raison d'être* to make its demands plausible, either a foreign enemy or an internal threat of subversion, so that the existence of armaments generates tension. 'In a circular fashion, the possession of weapons can intensify the factors that brought about their acquisition. Thus arms may increase the risk of conflict, strengthen national unity, and enhance the political position of the armed forces.'[2]

---

[2] *Ibid.*, p. 43.

There were plenty of causes around which the military could build up claims for their own requirements. The dissolution of the Pax Britannica lifted the lid from many ancient enmities, and new quarrels arose from drawing new frontiers. If one party to a dispute is armed, the other must arm too. If the forces in one or other get ahead, or believe they have got ahead, there will be no lack of an excuse for them to start making use of their weapons. The occasions for war are not the same thing as the causes of war; one of the main causes is the existence of armies. It is not only within the so-called free world that this principle applies. Disputes leading to armed conflict occur, in Africa and Indochina, between would-be socialist states.

Moreover, the possession of modern weapons does not only tempt the military to use them; it makes war far more destructive and cruel, for with sophisticated weapons goes the conception of 'total war' that has evolved in the West and wiped out all conception of honour and chivalry and all distinction between 'legitimate' military objectives and the destruction of the livelihood and the lives of the civilian population.

This curse has been laid upon the Third World by the great powers.

Apart from occasional wars, the main evil of modern armaments and the modern technology of surveillance is the extreme imbalance that they create between the power of authority and of the populace.

Capitalism grew up in the traditions of democratic liberalism and however much hypocrisy and ideological manipulation there may be in that tradition, it has meant that, with growing wealth, there has been a great diffusion of consumption and of education throughout the populations of the Western countries. There have been Factory Acts, limitation of hours of work, prohibition of child labour. Housing is not much to boast about, but cities at least provide sewage and clean water for almost every family, while the families of industrial workers have come to expect many formerly middle-class luxuries. Parliament and the press are free to criticise the authorities and the imposition of orthodoxy on intellectual life operates more through self-censorship than overt oppression.

When capitalism is transplanted into backward regions, it does not develop on these lines but (combined with growth of numbers) generates a trend towards increasing inequality and misery. Tyrannous governments are therefore necessary to hold society together. Any attempt to organise a labour movement is soon crushed and it is a commonplace for priests and intellectuals to be tortured to cure them of uttering dangerous thoughts.

Throughout human history, tyrants have established themselves by terror, but the special feature of tyranny today is that it is far more efficient than ever before now that it is equipped with modern technology. Moreover, the facility with which these instruments and methods can be acquired is a temptation to newly established governments, starting from some notions of legality, to take the road to tyranny.

Economic aspects

In so far as the arms trade influences the nature of regimes, it has an all-pervasive influence upon economic development. We must also consider its economic effects in the narrower sense of the use of resources.

It was calculated in 1970 that the overall GNP of Third World countries, taken together, had been growing since 1950 at 5 per cent a year, while their military expenditure grew at 7 per cent a year, and their imports of major weapons at 9 per cent.[3] About half of the foreign exchange cost is provided by donors. The rest is a burden on the countries' balance of payments.

With sophisticated armaments, even more than with consumer durables, 'import-saving' production adds to the foreign exchange bill because the cost of indispensable components comes to more than the cost of a complete article.[4]

When we discussed the relation of surplus to income we drastically simplified the problem of assuming that military and administrative expenses could simply be lopped off GNP so that we could examine the behaviour of the productive sector of the economy separately. Generally, no such calculation made is made either in the West or in the Soviet sphere. When military expenses are included, the meaning of GNP as a measure of the

[3] *Ibid.,* p. 83.
[4] Cf. p. 105 above.

flow of useful goods and services being made available to the population becomes all the more dubious.

The concepts of accumulation and 'national saving' also become ambiguous. We observed that to incur debt for importing luxury goods puts a drag on development; this is true *a fortiori* of acquiring means of destruction. Similarly 'import-saving investment' even when it does actually reduce the bill for imports, is substracting home resources from investment that could otherwise be useful. Investment in armaments adds even less to productive capacity if they are used than if they are idle while investment in basic industry makes it possible to increase investment and sets going the spiral of self-propelling growth.

It may be claimed that service in the armed forces contributes indirectly to economic development, since men are trained in discipline, hygiene and literacy, and learn to handle and repair mechanical apparatus. When they return to civilian life, they carry their skills with them. There is clearly some truth in this argument (though it is a sad comment on the social system inherited from imperialism that these benefits can be conferred only on the military) but it grows less true as the weapons grow more sophisticated and the skill involved more specialised.

In the developing world as a whole, it is estimated that military expenditure rose from $15 billion in 1960 to $39 billion in 1974 (at constant 1973 prices) while GNP *per capita*, on the same basis rose from $207 to $315;[5] that is to say while GNP *per capita* was multiplied by 1.5, military expenditure was multiplied by 2.6. This was not evenly spread. The largest increase was in the Middle East, which was a theatre of war during the period, but military expenditure rose also in what purported to be peaceful regions.

It is true that much of this outlay was subsidised by the developed countries, but that cuts both ways. If they had not been so much burdened by military expenditure both at home and for their clients, they might have been more generous with useful aid.

The military establishment limits civilian development not only directly by absorbing foreign exchange and scarce home resources and skills but also indirectly, through finance. In every country (not only in the Third World) there is a resistance against

[5] See Ruth Leger Sivard, *World Military and Social Expenditure,* 1976.

taxation. Revenue is limited by the capacity of the administration and the docility of the public. The amount of borrowing that can be undertaken without wrecking the financial system is also limited.

The inflationary effect of military expenditure is greater than that of outlay for productive purposes because it yields no product. Small quick-yielding investments bring an increase in output that counters inflation. A large slow-yielding investment, such as building a dam that will take five years to complete, is inflationary while it goes on but when it comes into use, it will bring a permanent increase in the flow of production. Military expenditure increases saleable production neither in the short run nor in the long.

The attempt to check inflation (even when it is not successful) limits government expenditure, which must be kept within bounds. The greater the burden that the military place upon the budget the less is available for productive or humanitarian uses.

In the developed Western countries, public expenditure on education is reckoned to be slightly greater than on so-called defence, but in education itself there is an element of cold-war competion, as is shown by the sudden expansions of universities in North America after the launching of the first sputnik. Unfortunately, 'defence' has not had an equally stimulating effect on the conquest of illiteracy in the Third World.

Research

Within the great powers and their respective satellites, science and advanced technology are largely devoted to developing means of destruction. This has also spilled over to the Third World. The scramble for atomic weapons absorbs the rare talent, training, and research facilities that might have been promoting economic and medical progress.

It is often observed that many valuable discoveries have been a by-product of military development. This does not apply to research in the Third World, which is devoted merely to applying discoveries made in the centres of power. In the centres themselves, it cannot be maintained that military research and development is a *better* way of discovering solutions for economic or medical problems than applying research to them directly.

The Chinese quickly entered the big league of atomic powers. After each successful test, a statement is issued that China would never be the first to use atomic weapons, calling upon all other powers to make the same declaration. Why do other governments refuse to do so? It is hardly likely that any one of them would feel bound by such a renunciation if it really was intending a 'first strike'. It must rather be that if all the major powers made such a declaration, the whole thing would appear absurd and the tax-payers in the West would revolt.

Even a genuine agreement to outlaw atomic weapons would not be a solution. For a long time, Hiroshima was the symbol of the ultimate horror, but nowadays worse chemical and biological horrors are being prepared, and 'delivery systems' have much improved.

Commercial trade

We observed that the export of arms to the Third World from the USA (like that from the USSR) was primarily induced by political motives, unlike that of other Western suppliers, who wanted export markets for their own sake. Recently, however, it seems that this is no longer true. After the cut-back of procurement for Vietnam, the great American corporations sought alternative outlets. In 1973, President Nixon waived a former restriction on the sale of modern sophisticated warplanes in Latin America. This opened up a promising market there. The sudden jump in oil revenues in 1973 put pressure on the balance of payments of all Western countries, increasing their need for exports, while at the same time providing funds for eager buyers. Thus the three years after 1973 saw the greatest arms race in recorded history and it shows no signs of slowing down (see p. 128). The market for arms, unlike all other markets, can never be saturated, for an increase in supply to one country in any region increases demand from its neighbours. The appeal to any one national supplier to refrain from acting as a 'merchant of death' is met by the argument: If we do not meet the demand, someone else will. Thus, at the present time, the prospects for a greater use of resources for humane and constructive purposes does not seem bright.

TABLE

Increase in the value of imports of major weapons by the Third World

	US $ millions, at constant (1973) prices		
	Average annual imports		
	1964–68	*1969–73*	*1974–75*
Total Third World	1521	2527	4387
Middle East	549	1181	2451
Far East, total	469	640	408
excluding Vietnam	259	266	332
South Asia	191	277	210
North Africa	70	98	378
Sub-Saharan Africa	130	126	401
Latin America	114	216	497

Source: *World Armaments and Disarmament*, SIPRI year book, 1976.

8

WHAT NOW?

During the so-called Decades of Development, 1950–70, there was an almost unbroken run of high employment and accumulation in the industrial capitalist economies. The great slump of the 1930s was a nightmare forgotten in the dawn of seemingly permanent prosperity. Effective demand was maintained largely as a by-product of cold and hot wars but there was a great increase in civilian wealth at the same time. Most of the Third World countries, through their connections with the capitalist world, experienced some growth of their national incomes in this period, while the mass of poverty and distress grew at the same time. Now those very connections have pulled them down into the capitalist slump.

The slump of the 1970s

There are important differences between the characteristics of the recession of the 1970s and that of the 1930s which affect its reaction upon what is now the Third World. First of all, as Kaldor has pointed out,[1] the relations between primary production and manufactures were quite opposite in the two cases. In the period 1925–29 the growth of primary production (partly as a result of technical progress in agriculture) exceeded the growth of consumption, so that there was an accumulation of stocks, which, with favourable expectations about future demand, could go on for years with only moderate falls in prices.

When the boom did break, prices fell catastrophically – by more than 50% in three years – and this, so far from stimulating the absorption of commodities by the industrial sector, had the very opposite effect; the fall in demand for industrial products coming from the primary producers, and the fall in

[1] See 'Inflation and Recession in the World Economy', *Economic Journal*, December 1976.

investment by the industrial countries in primary production – in opening up new areas, etc. – more than offset any stimulus to industrial demand on account of the rise in real incomes of the urban workers resulting from the fall in food prices: the rapid fall in commodity prices ushered in the greatest industrial depression in history.[2]

Contrariwise, during the period of high growth both in the West and in the Soviet sphere, demand gradually overtook supply for a number of commodities. Scarcities led to high prices even before OPEC took advantage of the chance to exercise its monopoly power. This precipitated a slump in industry, partly directly because a sudden increase in unspent profits deflated world demand and partly indirectly because the interaction of rising costs with rising wages brought on a violent all round rise of prices which led to strongly restrictionist measures, designed to counter inflation, being imposed all over the West.

As soon as industrial activity slackens, demand for materials falls, and relative prices come tumbling down again. Even OPEC was not able to maintain its terms of trade in real terms after the initial massive improvement. But now governments all over the Western world, bankers, and even public opinion, have seized upon the idea that inflation is a worse evil than unemployment. The fear that a revival of activity would lead to a new acceleration of inflation inhibits policies designed to revive effective demand.

There is a good deal of confusion in public discussion between the slump precipitated by the 'oil crisis' and the long-run problem of prospective scarcities of materials setting the 'limits to growth'. The slump causes a low level of utilisation of existing installations and, while it lasts, raw material prices relatively to industrial prices are kept low. Even for oil, real purchasing power fell sharply after 1975. The fear that material prices would rise again if activity recovered, and set inflation going again, is nothing to do with long-run prospects. Indeed, the prospect of long-run scarcities, in a rational world, should give a great boost to investment in finding substitutes and in devising less wasteful methods of consumption. Present unemployment is not due to lack of supply but to deficiency of demand.

Monetary restriction is made all the worse by competition between the Western nations. If they had shown good sense, they

[2] *Ibid.*, pp. 703–4.

would have agreed to share out the oil deficit amongst themselves and not allowed it to reduce home activity. But those which were still in surplus pushed all the deficit on to weaker competitors, which were therefore obliged to try to cut imports by the painful means of reducing the level of home employment. The temptation to use beggar-my-neighbour remedies became irresistible, and this led, in the first instance, to restricting imports from Third World producers.

The fall in earnings from sales of manufactures, and of raw materials, combined with the burden of debt service and the raised price of necessary imports of oil, dried up demand for manufactures from the non-oil Third World, and so deepened the slump in the West. Thus the whole world has once more got itself tied up in what Keynes in the 1930s used to call the humbug of finance.

A good part of oil proceeds began to be spent, mainly on armaments and spectacular buildings, and some was dribbled out in loans to poor countries but, for the non-oil Third World as a whole, demand for imports was severely restricted and, in 1978, there seems little prospect of the growth experienced before 1974 being resumed.

A change of slogans

Meanwhile, there has been a great revulsion against that type of growth. International institutions such as the World Bank and the ILO, as well as UNCTAD, and many research institutes and individual writers, point to the increase in misery that took place while so-called growth was going on.

Evidence of the persistence of poverty takes many forms. For example, the number of those unable to read and write has increased. The employment problem has remained intractable and in some areas may have become worse. Hunger and malnutrition are chronic and in parts of Asia and Africa periodic famines stalk the land. Perhaps most distressing is evidence, still incomplete but sufficiently strong that it can no longer be ignored, that in many countries the standard of living of the poorest members of the population has been falling absolutely.[3]

[3] Keith Griffin, 'Increasing Poverty and Changing Ideas about Development Strategies', *Development and Change* (Institute of Commonwealth Studies, Oxford.), Vol. 8.

Now the cry is for a change of direction and policies based upon meeting human needs. Such policies encounter formidable obstacles: 'It is obvious that the objectives of most Third World governments are inconsistent with the policies implicit in a basic needs strategy, namely, a sharp acceleration in the rate of growth combined with a radical redistribution of income and wealth.'[4]

Moreover such a strategy is inimical to the immediate interests of the transnational corporations who would find profitable markets for unnecessary commodities curtailed by it. Such vested interests pay only lip service to humanitarian ideals. Here we can do no more than discuss the measures that would be required for a 'frontal attack on poverty and unemployment', showing incidentally why they are not likely to be undertaken.

Agriculture is the foundation

From every point of view – political, economic and humane – the first necessity for the Third World is to increase production of basic foodstuffs.

This is a political objective, for a country which depends upon importing food must be subservient to the policies of its suppliers. After 1973, it was freely said in the United States: The Arabs have the oil weapon, but we have the food weapon. The food weapon can be used not only for political purposes but also to reinforce financial discipline. The indebtedness of the Third World has reached grotesque proportions, but repudiation is out of the question so long as countries can be threatened with famine if they break the rules of the international financial system.

Production of food is the most effective form of import-saving investment. For a country with a deficit on its balance of payments to import food means that it is borrowing in order to eat. The debt remains to be paid after the food has been eaten. This is the rake's progress that has led many Third World countries into the present impasse.

As we have observed, national boundaries, especially in the ex-colonial territories, do not correspond to viable economic entities; there are many nations for which to be self-sufficient in food seems an impossible ambition, but on a regional basis the

[4] *Ibid.*

problem could be solved. The 'non-aligned nations' have begun to talk of collective self-reliance. If the Third World countries could settle their historical and modern quarrels amongst themselves, and not allow themselves to be used as agents in the quarrels of the great powers, they could help each other out in economic development (as well as reducing the wastage of resources in maintaining armed forces to threaten each other).

Regional plans which consist merely in setting up a free-trade area generally have unfortunate effects, for the economies of the countries forming the group are not all equally strong. The one that is strongest to begin with offers the best opportunities for profitable investment, so that it grows stronger, attracts resources away from the others and retards their development instead of promoting it. When Third World governments embark on schemes of mutual aid to reduce their dependence on the West, it is necessary to take a great deal of trouble to ensure that the benefits of any scheme are genuinely mutual.

From the point of view of economic development, an increase in the production and consumption of food is a prime necessity. The Third World is carrying a huge reserve of potential labour in under-nourished people who are too weak to work hard. At the same time a great deal of protein is being wasted by being converted into meat. This is wasted twice over for the meat is fed to the wealthiest part of the community who do the least strenuous work.

The Latin-American type of agribusiness which monopolises great areas of land to supply profitable markets in the West[5] is now spreading, with the aid of air transport, into tropical Africa.

Seeing all the world as a global farm, agribusiness today is building on solid colonial tradition. Since the earliest outside interventions, agriculture in the colonized world has been seen as a mine from which to extract wealth rather than the basis of livelihood and nutrition for the local people. But today to the traditional 'export crops', like coffee, sugar and cocoa multinational agribusiness is adding items previously grown at home in the US or Europe: vegetables, strawberries, mushrooms, meat and even flowers.[6]

The balance between the sectors of the economy is a matter of the greatest importance from a humanitarian as well as a

[5] Cf. above, p. 37.
[6] J. Collins and F. M. Lappe (Institute for Food and Development Policy, San Francisco), *Social Scientist*, Trivandrum, October 1977, p. 5.

narrowly economic point of view. Industry developed in the West by gradually drawing workers out of an over-populated agriculture. This process has now reached its limit in England (not the British Isles in general) where agriculture is highly mechanised and, to keep a much reduced labour force on the land, wage rates have to compete with industry. Other capitalist countries are at various stages on the way to this development. In the Third World, labour is being expelled from agriculture faster than industry can absorb it. This happens both in the antiquated and in the modernising systems of agriculture. In the oppressive quasi-feudal system, cultivators are driven from the land because they cannot support their families on the incomes that they receive and in the modernising sector they are driven from land that is being concentrated into relatively large 'economic' holdings.

A frontal attack on mass poverty and unemployment requires an increase in the output of food but also an equalisation of consumption. The only way to combine both results is to go back to small-scale, labour-using agriculture and then to advance gradually from that base. But there seems to be little chance of such a drastic reversal taking place.

The basic requirements for a productive peasant agriculture have long been known : security of tenure, and a regular outlet for sales and supply of credit. Technical assistance is required, in the large – irrigation, electrification and lines of transport; and in detail – scientific experiment and education to solve problems as they arise rather than disseminating generalisations out of textbooks. Technical research should be directed to land-saving improvements – those which merely reduce labour per unit of product should wait until industry is ready to draw workers from the land into employment. But a redistribution of land, however drastic, does not provide a permanent solution. First, in a market economy, the process of polarisation would soon set in and re-create poverty for the less fortunate families. Second, there are many types of terrain in which small-scale operation cannot realise the potential productivity of the soil because the use of land, and especially of water, requires larger units of control. Third, the process of investment and technical progress goes on slowly with small units. The Chinese say: Agriculture is the foundation and industry is the leading factor. The industrialisation of agriculture begins with electrification and this requires a unit of control at least the size of a village to take advantage of the possibilities that it opens up. Some kind of cooperative or collective property in land and in means of production is necessary to provide a frame in which modernisation can go on without the polarisation between wealth and misery which it is bringing about all over the Third World today.

Sectoral distribution

However the organisational problems of production are solved, there would always be the problem of the relations between agriculture and the rest of the economy. First, in what way is a surplus to be taken from the agricultural sector to contribute to investment and to the general overhead of the economy? Second, what should be the terms of trade between the agricultural sector of the economy and the rest? Thirdly, how should the produce of agriculture be divided between exports and home consumption?

The first two problems, which are to a certain extent interconnected, present an inescapable dilemma. On the one hand, it is necessary to stimulate agricultural production by making it remunerative to the cultivator, which indicates high prices and low taxation. On the other hand, it is necessary to provide cheap food to overcome poverty and stimulate production in industry. Wealthy industrial countries can square the circle by subsidies – as in Japan – by buying staple crops from the cultivator at a higher price than they are sold to the public, or like the European Economic Community, throwing the burden on to industrial incomes by keeping food prices high, and leaving the workers to fight it out with their employers as to how the burden is divided between wages and profits.

Many developing countries, notably Egypt and India, have refrained almost entirely from taxing agricultural incomes, which cripples their fiscal system and allows much wealth to escape from contributing to government revenue. This policy arose from the desire to encourage agricultural production, based on the mistaken notion of treating it as a homogeneous sector of the economy. Capitalist farmers and rich peasants shelter behind the notorious poverty of the mass of cultivators to argue that agriculture cannot support taxation.[7] Immunity from taxation assists the process of concentration of wealth and landholding which is one of the influences that prevents agriculture from providing employment for growing numbers.

Industry, on which the bulk of taxes fall, is being obliged to subsidise agriculture, but a large part of the subsidy goes into the incomes of those who could well afford to pay their share. To remedy this situation requires a revolutionary change in the fiscal system which would be strongly resisted by those who have come to regard their privilege of immunity as a natural right.

Over and above the question of collecting a surplus from agriculture to contribute to national purposes is the question of the terms on which agricultural produce is transferred to other sectors of the economy, and, in particular, the problem of the relation of the price of food to industrial wage rates. In India, the policy has been to keep the price of grain high, while procuring a certain part of the crop for subsidised sales, through so-called fair-price shops, to relieve the worst poverty of the cities. This system benefits dealers, rich peasants and landlords, at the expense of the poorest part of the nation – the landless labourers.[8] (Only in one State, Kerala, does the public supply system attempt to cover the whole population.) In Egypt, a system of compulsory deliveries at low prices, designed to provide exports and cheap food for the cities, led to reduced supplies, because production was deflected into cash crops which were not strictly controlled. In the first case, the burden upon the industrial sector was partly wasted by allowing unnecessarily high incomes to a small proportion of the agricultural population; in the second case, the burden upon agriculture was set so high as to defeat its own purpose.

To find the pattern of prices that will induce the required pattern of cropping is a difficult matter. As long as there is even a partial free market, industrial materials and inessential luxuries command more remunerative prices than basic foodstuffs. This has been a notorious problem in the Soviet Union. Even in

[7] Cf. M. Abdel-Fadil, 'Intersectoral Terms of Trade, the Case of Egypt', WEP, 2–23/WP 39.
[8] Cf. Ashok Mitra, *Terms of Trade and Class Relations,* Frank Cass and Co., London, 1977.

China, where outputs are, in principle, controlled by quotas, the authorities have to keep an eye on the Communes to make sure that they do not put too much effort into crops that pay best, at the expense of grain. Perhaps it is impossible to find a perfectly satisfactory solution to all these problems, but to approach a solution it is evidently necessary to reduce inequality within the agricultural sector and to raise its level of productivity, which points once more to the basic problem of development – the need for reorganisation and technical improvement of the agricultural sector in the Third World.

The excessive dependence of Third World economies upon exports is a serious weakness but this does not mean that the output of exportable crops should necessarily be reduced. It means rather that production for home consumption ought to be increased.

As things are, the allocation of land to various uses depends upon the pattern of ownership and profitability so that the most fertile is often devoted to cash crops for export while the cultivators have to feed themselves somehow from the least fertile.

The poverty curtain

If the object of development is to overcome mass poverty, a great part of the effort that has been put into it has gone astray because of the waste of foreign exchange and the lopsided growth of industry that has come about from imitating Western patterns of consumption. It is very natural for the urban population in a colonial country, who have seen the standard of life of their foreign masters, who ride about in motor cars, to think that independence means that we shall have motor cars too. This conception helped to reinforce the inequality of consumption which already existed in the colonial countries and, as we have seen, to exaggerate inequality as economic growth began to take place in a distorted form.

A 'frontal attack on mass poverty' would require the countries of the Third World

to define for themselves the living standards or life-styles that they can afford on a nation-wide scale and which are consistent with their present state of overall poverty. It is inevitable that this would mean not only a much simpler standard of living, but a much greater concentration on public services which can be distributed more equitably – public buses, public hospitals, public education, even communal housing. If the developing countries really undertake such a sweeping change in their development strategies, the prestigious symbols of private ownership may also change – the familiar example being a bicycle economy instead of an automobile economy.[9]

Such a strategy would require a great change in the pattern of trade. The import of Western style luxury goods, and ingredients for producing them at home would be eliminated.

While machinery and raw materials would still figure prominently in the import budgets of the developing countries embracing the new development strategy, such imports would naturally be more limited when these countries increasingly improvise domestically and use whatever local resources and talents they have to look after their own problems. In other words, a 'poverty curtain' would descend across the developing world, isolating its development and trade from the traditional pattern.[10]

Industrial investment

The imposition of a poverty curtain, though it is advocated by a spokesman for the World Bank, is a somewhat idealistic conception. Its implications have been discussed, in the Indian context, in a more practical way by Professor Reddy.[11] He argues that a calculation of social cost–benefit shows that there are some basic industries which have been proved to require large-scale capital-intensive technology. These should be provided with the necessary investment. Other 'capital-intensive, labour-saving, luxury oriented, skill-demanding' synthetic based, large-scale mass-producing technologies' should be avoided, or the industries involved should be transformed 'so that they produce, for example, plants, machines, components, sub-assemblies or parts to be fed into rural industries'. (Electronics is mentioned as a promising field for this kind of development.)

Professor Reddy lists requisite principles as follows :

(1)   a preference for capital-saving and employment-generating, rather than capital-intensive and labour-saving, technologies;

[9] Mahbub ul Haq in *Trade Strategies for Development,* Paul Streeten (ed.), Macmillan, 1973, p. 100.
[10] *Ibid.*
[11] A. K. N. Reddy of the Department of Inorganic and Physical Chemistry, Indian Institute of Science, Bangalore, 'Towards an Indian Science & Technology', *Journal of Scientific & Industrial Research,* Vol. 32, No. 5, May 1973, pp. 207–15.

(2) a preference for cottage-scale and small-scale rather than large-scale technologies;

(3) a preference for the technologies of goods appropriate for mass consumption, rather than for individual luxuries;

(4) a preference for technologies requiring little skill or small modifications in the skills of traditional craftsmen like potters, weavers, blacksmiths, carpenters, cobblers, tanners and oil millers;

(5) a preference for technologies using local materials, rather than materials which have to be imported from abroad or transported from distant parts of the country;

(6) a preference for energy-saving, rather than energy-intensive, technologies;

(7) a preference for locally available sources of energy such as the sun, wind, and manure gas;

(8) a preference in the machine building and machine tool sector, for the technology of mass-producing, scaled-down, dispersable, miniaturized factories rather than the technology of mass-producing consumer goods;

(9) a preference for the technologies of *manu*facture rather than *machino*-facture;

(10) a preference for technologies which promote a symbiotic and mutually reinforcing, rather than parasitic and destructive, dependence of metropolitan industry upon the rural population.

This scheme of ideas would require some modification to be applied to those African economies which are at earlier stage of industrialisation, but the main principles are all the more important for them. In Latin America such teaching would fall on deaf ears and in India itself it meets with great resistance.

Professor Reddy's proposals involve 'walking on both legs' not only with respect to technology but also with respect to organisation; large-scale investment, in irrigation, the main provision of energy, some basic industries, and long-range transport should be provided by central authorities, while the bulk of consumer goods are produced by small-scale family business and cooperatives.

One can illustrate some features of the problem with the concrete case of the manufacture of dry cells used in torches and transistor radios. Today, barring the fabrication of the extruded zinc cans, the rest of the assembly of a dry cell can be done on a small scale. In fact, the Central Electrochemical Research Institute, Karaikudi, is offering the know-how for the manufacture of 1.8 million cells per annum by about 40 workers. It would take about thirty-three such producing units employing a total of 1650 workers to produce 60 million cells per annum. The current industrial licensing, however, is for large-scale factories each capable of producing 60 million cells per annum with only about *one-fifth* the number of workers. The point, however, is that the cells from the small-scale unit are not inferior performance-wise to the cells from the large scale factory. In fact, when one considers the poor half-life of dry cells at Indian ambient temperatures, the customer is more likely to get a 'full capacity' cell by bicycle distribution from a local producer than by rail-cum-truck transport from a distant factory. Hence, considering that 14 units have been recently licensed with a new extra capacity of 60 million cells each, one can see that the opportunity for the employment of about 20,000 extra people has been lost by the preference for large-scale production.

It should be stressed here that the scale of 1·8 million cells per annum is not the lowest possible scale. It is possible to go down to a cottage scale of 1500 cells per day by 10 workers. It is also possible, by suitable design of hand presses and mixers, to effect a drastic reduction of capital and generate a production technology which is not very different from that used by house-wives to make *murkus* [a kind of biscuit.][12]

The very fact that in this case the Indian authorities gave licences to large-scale business shows what obstacles lie in the way of reasonable proposals.

The economic system of family business is like that of small peasants. Family members work for a share in the income derived from sales – the distribution between wages and profits does not arise. Credit is needed to build up working capital in the first place. Thereafter their own savings go into improving their equipment as they evolve 'appropriate technology' for themselves with whatever help enlightened science can give them. Like peasants, they require a reliable market, which could be organised at the wholesale level. Since they are not committed to a narrow range of products by specialised machinery, their supplies are flexible and follow developments of demand without loss.

The merit of small-scale production is not so much that it is 'labour-intensive' and permits a rapid growth of employment as that it is 'capital-saving'. Since investible resources are scarce, they should be used where they tell most, that is where a high level of investment per man makes the greatest contribution to production, rather than wasted upon mechanising production merely to save labour. A symbiosis between nationalised industry where capital-using techniques are essential, and small-scale cooperatives or family business where they are not, is the fastest way to achieve full employment, and it is the most effective way to promote accumulation while at the same time providing for the 'human needs' of the population.

[12] *Ibid.*

Conceptions of this kind were advocated in the early discussions of national planning, for instance by Professor Mahalanobis in India, but when some public sector investment is injected into an economy where there is great inequality of income, the pull of the market becomes too strong for it. As in Brazil, heavy industry in the public sector ends by finding its outlet in supplying the requirements of the capital-intensive luxury production which the private sector finds most profitable.

In those parts of the Third World where industrial growth has flourished, the inequality of consumption has been built into the structure of investment and its very success is an obstacle in the way of organising the available labour force in each country to meet basic requirements for the whole population.

Social services

Of all human needs the most important, after an adequate diet, are education and the prevention of preventable disease. The top-heavy professional system of the West has been exaggerated in the Third World, so that streams of university graduates flow into a labour market that cannot employ them, in countries where a great proportion of the population is illiterate, and a few modern hospitals with all the latest sophistications are set up in cities where even the most elementary requirements for hygiene are not available in surrounding slums.

Inequality in provision of essential services has been cemented into the class structure of would-be developing nations as firmly as inequality in the consumption of luxury goods has been embedded in the structure of production. It would need an even greater wrench to redirect education to the benefit of society as a whole than to redirect industry to the requirements of mass consumption.

Demand management

One of the most striking achievements of the authorities in China is to have come through the years of harvest failure – 1959, 1960 and 1961 – without either famine or inflation. This was brought about by a system of rationing, and of keeping prices for the basic necessities stable at their former low level, while raising the prices of all inessentials high enough to mop up the excess of purchasing power.

These methods are not available to a country where trade is in private hands. A short-fall in supplies, or an expectation of a short-fall, causes hoarding both by dealers and by members of the public who can afford to stock up. Prices rise sharply. Industrial workers may be able to secure a sufficient rise of money wages to save them from outright starvation, but landless agricultural workers, and peasants whose holdings are too small to feed their families, are unable to survive. Famines, in modern times, are caused not by lack of food, but by lack of money to buy it.

Where the industrial sector is a large part of an economy, the rise in money wages and prices of manufactures due to a rise in food prices sets off an inflationary spiral. An initial rise in the price of food raises money incomes, increasing expenditure on food, which drives prices still higher and increases money incomes again.

A vicious spiral through the interaction of prices and money-wage rates has become endemic in the Western world. In order to try to combat it, the authorities resort to restrictive policies, cutting government outlay and raising interest rates, which curtail business investment and many other forms of outlay which are normally carried on with borrowed funds. This reduces employment and generally impoverishes the nations concerned, but once inflation has set in, it goes on feeding upon itself, and, so far, even the most savage deflationary policies have not been able to eliminate it.

The decline in activity in the West spills over to the Third World in a decline in the volume of exports of primary commodities, while the prices of imports (including oil) continue to rise. At the same time, the burden of debt service is absorbing a growing proportion of what export earnings the primary commodities can provide.

The moral for the Third World is still the same : to shelter behind a poverty curtain and make use of their own potential productive resources to meet their own basic needs.

International trade

The free-traders are fond of the expression : international division of labour. In the textbook model, with universal full employment of labour and other resources, balanced trade for each country and perfect competition in all markets, it is argued, in static terms (leaving out accumulation and technical change), that free trade tends to bring about the maximum possible level of production in the world as a whole, and that each country shares in it according to its level of productivity.

As we have seen, this has no relevance to actual conditions, but the argument is often applied to trade between the periphery, supplying raw materials, and the industrial centre. The principle of 'division of labour' is used to justify policies that hinder the efforts of the periphery to develop industry for itself.

The old argument has been transferred by the spread of the activities of transnational corporations. They are still concerned with extractive industries, but they are also engaged in exporting manufactures to Third World countries, partly through setting up assembly works close to markets and exporting components under the guise of 'import-saving' investment. Furthermore, the third stage of transnational activity, the use of cheap labour to supply exports to the centre itself, is spreading rapidly.

The 'international division of labour' between the periphery and the centre is now managed almost entirely by the great corporations. Competing amongst themselves, they are driven by the need to make profits, without regard to any interests but their own.

Conclusion

While population is still growing, though at a slightly decelerating rate, the arms race is continuing at an accelerating rate and the spread of commercialism is destroying human values everywhere, it is not easy to take an optimistic view of the situation of the Third World today. All that economic analysis can hope to contribute is to remove some illusions and to help whoever is willing to look to see what their situation really is.

INDEX